Praise for *Leader Business*

"We have worked with Tom Magness for several years and have found his leadership blog to speak right to the needs of our company. Even in our industry (fashion), leadership is leadership. I encourage everyone to buy this book and apply Leader Business *to their personal and professional life. His insights are already paying off for me—and for our company."*

– Suzanne Lerner, Co-Founder, Michael Stars, Inc.

"Finally, someone has written an easy to follow guide to leadership that provides a specific method and path for success. Plus it is a fun read. I've worked with Col. Tom Magness for over 20 years. He is known throughout the Army as our premier trainer and one of our finest leaders. He's combined his enviable knowledge of leadership and leading with his unique and world-class training expertise to deliver a profound and simple guide. This book is for anyone who wants to learn the business of leading."

– Major General (ret.) Randy Castro

"Col. Magness exemplifies in his writings his real concept of what true leadership is all about: action, not just words. Tom embodies the best of the best. I applaud his decision to put forth an easy-to-understand framework; he not only believes it, but follows it. He will surely guide and inspire even those who do not feel they can be leaders."

– U.S. Representative Grace F. Napolitano

"Tom Magness shows us how, at a time when the world is experiencing a serious leadership vacuum, we can use the battle-tested structure of the military planning and execution process to restore and invigorate fundamental leadership responsibilities and principles."

– Guy Greco, Senior Partner, Virtual CEO Consulting Group

"Leaders lead with heart, courage, and conviction to earn the hearts and minds of those they lead. Tom Magness has made a career out of showing our American servicemen and women how to live and lead as he has done—and in the end they are better people for it. Now you can learn firsthand from a master of leadership how to be the kind of leader you want to be. His stories are thought-provoking, his words are inspirational, and his strategies for making you a better leader are some of the best you will ever read."

– Steve Harper, Author of *The Ripple Effect: Maximizing the Power of Relationships For Your Life and Business*

"With his experience at the leadership laboratories of West Point and the National Training Center, Tom Magness provides an excellent flight plan for emerging leaders as well as for seasoned veterans in their quest for constant improvement. Read Tom's book and subscribe to his blog. Make Leader Business *a part of your plan for success."*

– John Michael Magness, Author of *Pilot Vision*

Second Edition

Leader Business

Second Edition

Leader
Business

Battle-Tested Leadership
Strategies For Any Organization

Thomas Henry Magness

LBI
PUBLISHING

ISBN: 978-0-615-37618-9

Library of Congress Control Number: 2010907948

Printed in the United States of America

Layout: Think Write Communications
             www.think-write.net

Cover design: Mac McCrary Design
                www.macmccrary.com

                brandaround
                www.brandaround.com

LBI Publishing
Los Angeles, CA

Stay connected with Leader Business at
www.leaderbusiness.blogspot.com.

*Dedicated to the men and women who voluntarily
put themselves in harm's way . . . and to those who lead them.*

Table of Contents

Acknowledgments

I am a leadership work in progress and a testimony to the fact that leaders are made, not born. I spent four years immersed in the role of teacher/mentor/leadership coach at the U.S. Army's National Training Center (NTC) at Fort Irwin, California. I've held 16 leadership positions in 25 years of commissioned service and have served as commanding officer at the company, battalion, and brigade level. I have led small and large units ranging from 15 to 800+ and have had the privilege of working around the world with professional warriors, both military and civilian, in peacetime and in combat. But I could not have done any of this without an extraordinary group of people helping me understand what right looked like when it came to leadership.

I have served with and for some great military leaders who have given me insights into the business of leaders. I have tried my best to learn from them and I know that each, in their own way, has shaped how I lead today. Among them were great warrior leaders like: Jack O'Neill, Andy Aadland, Bruce Scott, Bruce Porter, Chuck Honore, Marc Coats, Russ Lachance, Rock Marcone, John Kem, Joe Fucella, Jack Grubbs, and Chris King. I have worked with several great leaders who continue to serve including BG Brian Watson, BG Ed Cardon, MG John Peabody, MG Bill McCoy, LTG Mark Hertling, GEN J.D. Thurman, LTG Bob Cone, LTG Rick Lynch, and LTG Bob Van Antwerp. I have also learned from a great group of professional soldiers and noncommissioned officers with whom I have served. To each of them, I say thanks for your selfless service, for having the patience to mentor me, and for all of your assistance throughout my career.

I have been fortunate to have one senior leader take a particular interest in my growth and development. Retired Army Major General Randy Castro has given me consistently wise counsel since we served together in Germany in the early 90s. He continues to shape the way I think about things like vision and passionate leadership today. It is one thing to have a mentor who can provide professional advice. It is another level altogether when you can call that person a friend. Randy has been both to me.

No assignment shaped my thinking about leadership the way my tour of duty at Fort Irwin, California did. To the Sidewinder Team at the Army's National Training Center, I thank each of you for the way you modeled the Army's values. Most people will never understand the quiet professionalism each of you brought to your jobs as Observer Controllers in the unforgiving Mojave Desert. I learned from you what it means to be a "brother." You are great and mighty warriors and I am humbled to wear the same Sidewinder belt buckle as you.

To the civilians of the Army Corps of Engineers with whom I have served in Detroit, Los Angeles, and Afghanistan, you have my absolute respect for all that you do. You put the "brand" on each and every project and serve the nation in incredible ways. And while you do so without much thanks, I offer up my heartfelt appreciation for all that you have done—for me and for the Army. I have learned that good engineering plus leadership can positively affect people's lives. You have taught me volumes about both.

No project like this would be possible without great friends and a great team pushing me across the finish line. Anne got me started—one chapter per month—many years ago. JoAnn has proofread each chapter and motivated me to finish the job. Thanks to both of you for believing in the message.

Many others have given me feedback on my writing, whether in articles or at the Leader Business blog, and have encouraged me to get this done. You know who you are. Thanks to each of you from the bottom of my heart.

Steve Harper, aka "The Ripple Dude," convinced me that I could do this project and connected me with his publishing team. He has my sincere appreciation for his mentorship on the project and for providing the means for distribution. Ripple on, Steve. Marc Schwarz at Think Write Communications has been a patient project manager for this work. His efforts have transformed a bunch of words into a final product that I hope he is proud to put his name against. Thanks, Marc, for your assistance in editing, layout, printing, and everything else it took to make this into an actual book. Lastly, thanks to Mac McCrary for help with graphics and the good people at Thomson-Shore for printing. It definitely took a village to help raise this project. I look forward to collaborating with you all on future efforts!

Finally, I want to thank those whose unconditional love and support have inspired me to write this book. Thanks to my Mom and Dad for teaching me about leadership and character at a young age. While my Dad is not with us, I know he has been cheering me on to be a better leader as part of the "cloud of witnesses." I hope I made him proud. I have been blessed with many leadership role models inside my own family from my sister Jen, brothers Paul and John, uncles who have all served in the military, in-laws who have taught me about selfless service, grandparents, cousins, and all the rest. I love you all. Thanks especially to brother, businessman, leader, and "best selling author" John Magness for inspiring me to write my own book. After seeing how difficult it was to get this completed, I am humbled with what you have done with *Pilot Vision*—simply amazing.

I appreciate more than anything else what my three girls have done to support my various projects, initiatives, deployments, late nights, and everything else that comes with being a military family. To my wife Michelle, you are an amazing leader in your own right. I am so blessed to have you in my life and know I don't deserve you. Thank you for supporting me in this project. You're the best and I love you. To my beautiful daughters, Jenna and Shelby, you all give me examples of leadership every day. I love you and thank you for helping me in my journey to learn about the business of leaders. God has definitely blessed me in countless ways, beginning with placing all three of you in my life.

I end these acknowledgments in the same manner as I started: I am a leadership work in progress. By no means should the completion of this book suggest that I have figured it all out. I am as flawed as anyone else—perhaps more so! But with the encouragement of family and friends, and the redemption that is available to all of us, I keep getting up and striving to do my best. I give God all the glory and stand upon the claims of Philippians 4:13: "I can DO all things through Christ, who strengthens me."

Preface to the Second Edition

I originally wrote *Leader Business* prior to my final tour of duty in the military. I had lessons to share and I did not think I should wait before sharing these concepts with those who might benefit from them. Based on the feedback that I have received since the initial printing, and the hundreds—even thousands—of leaders who have been inspired to add the principles of *Leader Business* to their leadership toolbox, I am glad I did not wait.

Fortunately, however, I had one final opportunity to apply the *Leader Business* approach, one final mission while still in uniform: deployment to Afghanistan. The specific challenges and lessons of that deployment are not covered in this book. But what I can assure you is that the principles articulated here were once again "battle-tested." And once again, they proved their worth.

I recall very clearly the day one of my teammates in Afghanistan walked in with my book in their hands. I felt like a proud papa! It truly is a great feeling to see one's ideas finally on paper, bound and ready for public consumption in the "arena of ideas."

It can also be a slightly unsettling feeling. I knew that I better walk the talk like never before. The last thing I wanted was to have one of my employees come up to me and say, "I notice that on page 132 you said we should do X, so why are we doing Y?" No, I didn't need that challenge to my credibility! I knew I needed to be intentional and consistent in how I applied the principles of *Leader Business*.

By the end of my time in Afghanistan, I had spent more than a year "down range" with the Army Corps of Engineers validating the approach on these pages. In other words, I tested them on the ultimate field, with the highest of stakes . . . and they work.

Deployment is difficult, no question. Seven days a week for over a year, each of those days long and exhausting and filled with immense physical, emotional, and mental challenges. The experience simply confirmed the fact that leadership is the ultimate difference-maker. It is the difference between success and failure, good and great—even between life and death. It all comes down to leadership.

When I arrived in Afghanistan, it was as part of the President's "surge," with the size of the U.S. forces there rapidly increasing. As such, it was never a better time to be in the construction business. But with a clear eye toward finishing the mission and withdrawing from that country, the surge translated into a huge spike in what my organization was asked to do. Essentially, we went from a $1 billion construction program to a nearly $4 billion one. We needed to build infrastructure, educate our Afghan teammates about how to take over from us (whether to keep building the infrastructure or to maintain what we transferred to their control), and finish the job.

While this isn't the place to dive deeply into the lessons we learned, I will tell you that it came down to leadership. People wanted to be included in planning, especially if I was going to ask more of them. They wanted not only to be challenged, but also to be connected to the purpose of the organization. They wanted to know that their contribution was aligned to the mission. They wanted to learn and grow, be responsible for their output, and be recognized when they did well. And these principles proved just as valid when leading (through influence) our Afghan partners as they did with the American "troopers" in my command. In sum, all people responded favorably when led in accordance with the principles of this book.

History will be the judge as to whether we have accomplished anything of lasting value in Afghanistan. In my mind, and I believe by any measure of success, the team that I was fortunate enough to lead performed superbly. I loved every minute in command of those amazing military and civilian team members who made up the Corps of Engineers in Kabul, Afghanistan, and I am proud of what we did. I am equally proud of how we executed our mission with and through our Afghan partners, many of whom I still call friends. You may not hear much about what we accomplished; in fact, most of what we did was never—and likely will never be—reported. But as you will learn in Chapter 11, it is not about "hooah," but about "dooah!" And I believe that my outfit got it done.

These principles work. They have the power to transform individual leaders and the organizations they lead. They truly are the sort of battle-tested leadership strategies that can help your team go from good to great.

As far as book number two and the specific stories and lessons from Afghanistan, I'm working on that! But just as you wouldn't want to study business strategy without a good understanding of fundamental economics, you'll want to read this book, focusing on the *fundamentals of leadership*, first. So, dig in here and let's go to work on the tactics and the principles of leadership that I call *Leader Business*.

Introduction

The Business of Leaders

"Leadership is action, not position."
Donald H. McGannon

If the 1980s have remained in the public consciousness as the "decade of greed," then it's likely that the first 14 years of the 21st century will be remembered as the "decade of leaderlessness." For all the advances in technology ushered in by the new millennium, our leadership deficit, in both corporate and civic life, has never been more evident. In virtually every facet of our society, we see a growing gap between the demands of leadership and the readiness of those in charge. Consider just a few of the unmet challenges of the past few years:

• Companies found that they could see their stock prices shoot up to unprecedented levels simply by adding ".com" to their title. Until the bubble burst in early 2000, that is. Then we realized that companies needed to have viable business plans, that revenue mattered, that a qualified, experienced management team was necessary before throwing away millions at free-spending 20-somethings with cool Super Bowl commercials! Bold, aggressive risk-taking had to be mitigated; visions had to be coupled with detailed plans and analysis; and results mattered.

• The revelations of fraudulent accounting practices by Enron, Arthur Andersen Consulting and WorldCom in 2001-02 shed light on the lack of accountability among multi-billion dollar enterprises, shattering investor faith and devastating employees' retirement funds even as company leaders like Enron CEO Kenneth Lay raided the corporate coffers and pleaded ignorance about the actions of their subordinates.

• September 11, 2001 found a nation and its leaders ill-prepared for the intentions of those who would do her harm. Countries around the world acted surprised to learn that such evil existed, yet clearly lacked the coordinated decision-making and synchronized intelligence infrastructure to prevent such calamities.

• In 2005, Hurricane Katrina revealed the difficulties of leading in crisis, especially with inadequate preparation. Federal, state, and local teams lacked coordination or a well-rehearsed plan, and as a result operated with staggering inefficiency. The only bright spot? A U.S. Army general finally demonstrated the importance of straight talk, decisive action and leadership in crisis, helping New Orleans emerge from what could have been an even worse catastrophe. All fingers pointed outward and no one accepted responsibility for poor preparation and inept execution.

• The collapse of financial markets in 2008 once again highlighted leadership shortcomings—this time with literally trillion-dollar implications! Both business and political leaders demonstrated an appalling lack of foresight in permitting unqualified applicants to qualify for risky home loans. Gimmicks like bundling, zero-down and interest-only mortgages, and balloon payments seemingly raised no flags among the supposed overseers, perhaps because they were too busy collecting both actual and political capital from an obviously broken system.

• Never was political leadership more polarizing than in 2009-2010. Deficits grew exponentially across the United States. Trillion dollar bills became law without consensus (and without being read, but that is another issue). People talked of hope, but not about the *actions* that would be required to build consensus, align resources, and develop sustainable alternatives. Politicians spoke of values such as courage and loyalty, yet failed to represent their constituents on issues of war and peace, financial and personal health, and the use and preservation of our resources. These are our leaders?

Even in much smaller arenas, we see similar shortcomings: incompetent leaders who have no real understanding of the organizations they lead; managers who communicate only by email and know nothing of empowerment, time management, decision making, or leader development; supervisors who repeat the same mistakes time and again; and most troubling, leaders who cannot set priorities, miss milestones, mismanage resources, care little for those they lead, and do not accomplish their mission.

Too many of today's organizations—both large and small—are rudderless ships helmed by visionless navigators. And too many of today's leaders equate vision with flowery rhetoric while lacking even a basic understanding of the principles of planning and execution that transform vision into reality. As for genuine inspiration, risk-taking, or difference-making . . . forget about it.

It seems that everywhere we look—in our factories, our hospitals, our schools, and in our communities—we see leaders coming up short. Business executives seemingly care only about themselves. Community leaders fail under duress and during times of crisis. Political leaders do not appear to understand consensus building, communication, long range planning or risk mitigation, and cannot admit failure as a first step in self-examination and learning. Employees are uninspired, underdeveloped and unappreciated. We clearly have a leadership deficit.

Yet for all the talk in recent years about organization culture, social networks, flat organizations, and a new breed of workers (Generations X, Y, and Z), the reality is that leadership still matters. In fact, it may be more critical than ever. For most of us, it is the basis for whether or not we enjoy our jobs . . . and whether we stay or depart for greener pastures. For any organization, it is often *the* difference between success and failure.

So where are the leaders? Where are the people who are rooted in reality, who are able to effectively translate words into goals, goals into objectives, objectives into executable tasks, and tasks into real results? Where are the leaders who can transform hope into lasting change? Where are the bold, aggressive risk-takers who see two and three moves ahead of everyone else? Where are the managers who make work fun, who inspire greatness, and who foster camaraderie and teamwork?

The fact is that *we* must be those people. We are the ones who must become the leaders we desperately want, the leaders we absolutely need. Even if you've never had much in the way of formal leadership training, it's never too late to acquire the principles that characterize effective, inspiring leaders. This book is designed to help you do just that. If there's one thing I've learned in a lifetime of leadership, it's that leaders aren't born. They are grown—one step, one event, and one mistake at a time. Mission successes and failures both serve as opportunities for introspection, providing insights on means to improve. Advancements bring prospects of becoming a *better* leader, not a *bigger* one.

So whether you're new to this "leadership thing" or just in need of a refresher course, buckle up and get ready to learn from one of the world's elite leadership universities, the U.S. Army, and a number of other institutions who grow people who demonstrate every day what leaders *do*.

Leader Business

As a young Army lieutenant, I was once counseled by my commanding officer about the poor maintenance status of my platoon's vehicles and equipment. "Not my problem," I told him. "Talk to the mechanics in the motor pool."

"Son," the colonel explained, "this is *leader business*. I need you to get in there and make something happen. Accomplish the mission. Got it?" Leadership lesson number one: You can delegate authority and specified tasks to others, but you cannot delegate the burdens of command or the overall responsibility to lead. Bottom line: no matter how much we delegate, we are still in charge.

The Colonel would later use this same term, "leader business," to describe my responsibilities with regard to counseling and developing subordinates, to continuously focus on learning and self-development, to accomplishing the mission, to taking care of soldiers and their families—as well as a host of other topics. To be an effective leader, I was frequently told, I needed to step up, make a difference, and understand the full range of tasks associated with this leader business. I needed to learn quickly what leaders do to make all these things happen.

The problem was, no one ever really defined leader business for me. Over time, I gained insight into it whenever my CO said something like "This is leader business" or "That is leader business." Sometimes I heard about it when I made a mistake or neglected it. Perhaps more importantly, I learned from watching others what leader business was NOT.

Until my retirement in 2011, I held 17 leadership positions in 26 years of commissioned service. I have served as commanding officer at the company, battalion, and brigade level. I have led small and large units ranging from 15 to 800 employees and have had the privilege of working around the world with professional warriors, both military and civilian, in peacetime and in wartime. I have served on a variety of staffs, both as a team leader and a team member. I even spent four invaluable years as a trainer/coach at the U.S. Army's National Training Center (NTC) at Fort Irwin, California, a virtual leadership laboratory in some of the most demanding conditions and pressure-packed scenarios that could be devised.

What perhaps makes my journey unique from other professional soldiers is the combination of this time as a leadership consultant at the NTC with my subsequent assignments in non-traditional, mostly civilian organizations with the Army Corps of Engineers. In those roles I was much more of a CEO than an all-powerful unit commander, charged with balancing billion-dollar budgets and working with contractors, stakeholders, tribes, and members of Congress. I have held town hall meetings, press conferences, and public hearings. I have made important decisions on issues as diverse as water supply, development permits, overhead accounts, and the hiring and firing of team members.

Through these diverse experiences, I've learned that the leadership principles utilized by the military apply just as well in the private sector. I may not have it all figured out, but I have a pretty good idea now what my first commander meant. Leader business is universal—and universally important—whether you're commanding a battalion, managing a department, or running a small business. Regardless of where we serve, it is about what we do in fulfilling the responsibilities that are uniquely ours as leaders. There is a gap. People are counting on us to fill it.

A Leadership Journey

Leadership is a verb. It is not a goal achieved after years of diligent labor. It is not a destination; it's the journey itself. It is the process of persistence, passion, and absolute commitment to excellence. It involves a willingness to roll up one's sleeves and to do the hard, sometimes thankless work that makes a difference in an organization. Leadership is the crucial difference between right and wrong, winning and losing, good and great.

Some promote the notion that the goal of successful leadership is to produce more followers. I believe that the goal of leadership is to accomplish the mission, producing *successful* followers while growing more *leaders*. Leadership is about people. Good leaders, both military and civilian, understand that their principal role is to motivate, inspire, and lead . . . people. Missions should be designed to make best use of the skills and talents of . . . people. New technologies are acquired as enablers for . . . people.

I learned this early in my career while at the Army's primary small unit leadership training venue, the U.S. Army Ranger School at Fort Benning, Georgia. I did not have the best grasp of foot-soldier procedures and knew little about infantry tactics and combat operations in the swamps, mountains, and desert conditions that were inherent to Ranger training. And I certainly didn't receive the coveted "Ranger Tab" on the strength of my parachute jumps and pathetic landings!

Instead, I focused on leadership. I could issue quality instructions to my team. I understood the importance of time management, delegation, and risk mitigation. I knew how to prepare my team for the mission, how to conduct quality rehearsals, and how to make decisions. I was good at operating under pressure and accomplishing the mission. While others succumbed to the stress of constant evaluation and days without food or sleep (we had only about a 40% graduation rate), I excelled. I stayed positive, took care of my men, and leveraged the leadership skills I had learned at West Point and in my previous assignments.

Thirteen years later, the primacy of mission- and people-focused leadership was validated during my assignment as commanding officer of the Army Corps of Engineers district in Detroit, Michigan. After just one week in my new position, I sat down with my family, head in my hands, and bemoaned my fate. I was a combat engineer, I complained, not a CEO—especially one charged with overseeing hundreds of projects, more than 500 civilian employees, an area of coverage that included all or part of five Great Lakes states, and an annual budget of over $100 million. It sure seemed that the professional engineers, scientists, lawyers, and support staff, many of them with more time in the Army Corps than I had on the planet, could get by just fine without me. Someone in the Army Assignment Office had surely screwed up!

Then it hit me—this wasn't about me, wasn't about whether the assignment was the right command for me. It was about whether I was going to step up and be the right commanding officer—the right leader—for my new team. Five hundred people, regardless of their individual skills, won't lead themselves. They needed to stay focused on the mission, to be trained, to be rewarded, and to be empowered. They needed to know the big picture. They needed a leader who could see over the horizon. I realized that I wasn't being sent to this new command just to be an engineer; I was being sent to determine how to make my engineers successful.

Leaders provide the energy to make excellence possible. They sacrifice, providing blood, sweat, and tears, because they care about the organization and its people, and the respective success of both. They are servants whose hopes and dreams are tied to the successes of each member of the team. They are team players, focused on the health of the team and their ability to accomplish the mission. They make everyone feel appreciated while seeking to increase the value of each team member.

Bridging the Leadership Gap

With that in mind, allow me to make the case for bridging our current leadership gap using battle-tested principles drawn from the profession of arms. This is not just some self-serving theory, either. The John F. Kennedy School of Government at Harvard University annually publishes its "National Study of Confidence in Leadership" based on surveys and interviews conducted across the nation. The leadership skills and attributes of the military consistently exceed those of any other profession or business sector. Our men and women in uniform get high marks in the areas of personal and professional character, charisma, crisis response, decisiveness, taking charge, empathy, communication skills, and building consensus.

Obviously, there are some challenges associated with translating pure military lessons into a business or civilian environment. Twenty-first century business battlefields are networked, team-centric, and faced with continually-shifting boards of directors, shareholders, customers, price points and profit margins. They are usually not suited for top-down, hierarchical, command-and-control, "hooah" leadership. Business, while often combative, is not combat. That said, in any setting, on any battlefield, people are *still* people, and leadership is *still* leadership. The principles don't change; what's effective in the tactical world has been validated in the real world. My own leadership journey has given me the basis to confirm these findings.

Now it's time for *your* first mission, time to jump feet-first into the nuts and bolts of *Leader Business*. Turn the page and let's get started!

Chapter 1

A Battle-Tested Strategy

"Some people dream of success, while others
wake up and work hard at it."
ANONYMOUS

Lieutenant Colonel Steve Brown was in a fix. Since 0300 that morning, he had lost almost half of his 800-man task force. His casualties and damaged vehicles needed immediate evacuation, while his remaining troops were low on ammunition and water. It was painfully clear that the attack against a fortified enemy position to the north of Medina Wasl had stalled. It was decision time—should they sit tight and wait for reinforcements, abandon the mission and return to base, or continue the fight?

He asked his staff for their thoughts. Just once he wanted his team to demonstrate at least some rudimentary analysis and present some legitimate recommendations rather than simply parroting what he already knew. Instead of being inside the enemy's decision cycle, all too often Lt. Col. Brown felt like he and his staff were far, far outside it. It seemed that his intelligence officer was always two steps behind the enemy, and his "current ops" section seemed unaware that the incidents they were painstakingly tracking had already been superseded by new events. Making matters worse, his communications were abysmal. The only thing he could be sure of was that neither he nor his staff had a timely and accurate picture of what was really happening on the battlefield.

If there was a bright side to any of this, it was that this wasn't a real mission; it was an exceedingly realistic training scenario at the

Army's National Training Center in the desert near Ft. Irwin, California. Still, that comfort didn't keep Lt. Col. Brown from asking his tank driver to dig out an industrial-size bottle of Motrin—this day wasn't going to get any shorter.

What really stung was that Lt. Col. Brown knew he was ultimately responsible for the poor performance of his staff, many of whom were new to the unit. He had not trained them as well as he should have. He had not integrated them smoothly into their respective teams. Even knowing the operational risks (especially given the lack of good routes and the density of the urban area through which they would have to pass), he had failed to consider mitigation measures in sufficient detail. The lack of synchronization painfully underscored his failure to demand a rehearsal to work out the bugs in the plan. He fretted about constantly having to "pull" information, but he was forced to admit that he had never made his information requirements clear to his team.

One thing at least was certain—there would be a lot of "teachable moments" in the post-mission After-Action Review. Lt. Col. Brown grimly conceded that his NTC coach was right: "Life be hard in the desert!"

The preceding vignette gives only a glimpse of some of the challenges that leaders experience at the Army's National Training Center (NTC), which are themselves just a cross-section of the issues addressed daily by thousands of U.S. military personnel around the world. There is never enough time to do things perfectly. Plans are never fully developed and never completely staffed. Personnel shortages make operating at peak efficiency a dream. Resources are rarely available where and when needed. And regardless of what decision the leaders make, the competition (the enemy) always gets a vote.

Brigade-sized units rotate through the NTC to train for 14 consecutive days in simulated combat operations. It's the most intense training experience the Army can offer its units and their leaders. Located on a piece of terrain roughly the size of Rhode Island in the heart of the Mojave Desert, the maneuver area (affectionately known as "the box") is the practice field for combat units to conduct full-contact scrimmages against the crack Opposing Force (OPFOR). It's demanding, exhausting, and realistic leadership training. (I believe General J.D. Thurman coined the expression, "Life be hard in the desert" in accounting for the challenges that every day in "the box" presented to unit leaders. The infamous corollary, "It's even harder when you're stupid!" was probably established when he saw some of my own bone-headed training maneuvers!)

At its core, the NTC is a virtual leadership laboratory. Harsh terrain and weather, both marked by extremes, make every day, every event, a case study. Each decision provides opportunities for insights on organizational behavior and leadership, with hundreds of data points on units from crew (2-4 soldiers) to brigade (3500+). Leadership styles, decision-making, motivation of subordinates, vision, command climate, character, employee relations—these challenges are on display every day at the NTC and ripe for investigation.

Plan ▸ Prepare ▸ Execute ▸ Learn

The framework for *Leader Business* is based on the typical mission cycle for a military unit, one that I observed hundreds of times, and one that I believe is the basis of any leadership endeavor. Let's assume that a tactical unit plans, prepares, and executes a mission every 24-48 hours. At the completion of each operation, its members then participate in a focused self-examination period, collect lessons learned, and begin the next mission planning cycle. To add to the complexity, at any given point a unit might be involved in different phases of multiple, simultaneous missions: planning one, preparing a second, executing yet another.

Sometimes this cycle is compressed into a much shorter period, sometimes a longer one. The business equivalent would be developing and executing a business plan or going through a product life-cycle every 1-2 days. It's like taking an entire fiscal year for a company, compressing it into two days, and capturing the key lessons for subsequent application. That is essentially what the NTC is able

to provide the forces training there—and why the lessons observed there are so ripe for harvest and application.

One of the results of this harvest is the four-stage framework for *Leader Business* shown at the top of this page:

1. ***Leaders Plan:*** Leaders set the condition for success by providing the necessary input to develop an executable roadmap.

2. ***Leaders Prepare:*** They enable success by preparing themselves and their teams for the mission.

3. ***Leaders Execute:*** They complete the mission and create wins for their team.

4. ***Leaders Learn:*** Finally, leaders enable learning through activities before, during, and after each event.

Every step in this cycle requires specific actions by competent leaders of character in order to be successful. It is within this framework that we can see and define the roles, responsibilities, and unique deliverables of the leader. As a coach at the NTC, I could "peel back the onion" of challenges experienced during mission execution and point to a specific leader action, or a failure to take action, that was the major causal factor. What did the leader do, or fail to do, that produced the observed outcome?

Sometimes this can be difficult to swallow. Do I mean that everything is the leader's fault? Well . . . yeah, pretty much. Leaders build and prepare the team, assign the work, and manage execution. They are responsible for both individual and organizational learning. Determining where things go wrong usually starts with an examination of the leader. That's why we get paid the big bucks, right?

Part I of *Leader Business* covers the leader's responsibilities with regard to planning. It begins with the leader's role in defining the future, inspiring the team to greatness, and creating a shared vision. We hear a great deal about "vision" these days, but if anything its importance as a unique responsibility of a leader is still underrated. It is absolutely the most critical element of any journey: identifying the destination. Leaders must similarly understand their points of input in the planning process. *Leader Business* uses the battle-tested structure of the military's decision-making process to provide a guide to a leader's responsibilities in planning and decision making. Once a vision is developed and a roadmap is created . . . well, that's when capable, mature leaders really make their money. They build consensus, mitigate and manage risk, and align the team. They ensure that the vision, the plan, and the resources necessary for both, are correct and in place.

In Part II of *Leader Business*, we deal with how leaders enable success by preparing themselves and their team for battle. Before the plan can be executed, subordinates must be developed, teams must be built, assignments must be handed out, and rehearsals must be completed. Leaders manage the clock and ensure that priority activities are accomplished. Preparation is the critical phase during which leaders ensure that the plans and strategies have been appropriately understood down to the lowest levels, that adequate resources have been distributed, and that folks are generally prepared to do what we want and need them to do.

Part III focuses on doing what we get paid to do—accomplishing the mission, satisfying the customer, and creating shareholder and stakeholder value. We will discuss communication, empowering subordinates, and situational awareness as critical enablers of mission accomplishment. We will address those elements that are the mark of effective leaders: execution, decisiveness, and the ability to lead during times of crisis.

Finally, in Part IV of *Leader Business*, we will highlight the leader's responsibilities with regard to continuous improvement. We'll look at how to incorporate After Action Reviews (AARs) into the operational battle rhythm, and why doing so is such a critical driver for success. We will examine how to train our team and how to serve as a leader/coach for both individual and organizational learning.

Near the end of each chapter is, appropriately enough, a section called "Leader Business." These are what we call Tactics, Techniques, and Procedures, or TTPs. They are suggestions on how to apply the topics addressed in the respective chapters to our leadership. They include specific applications that highlight what might work for those endeavoring to incorporate these leadership issues.

Each chapter ends with "Marching Orders," a set of leading questions designed to promote further study and self-reflection. A suggested way to leverage them would be to meet as small groups and review one chapter at a time, using the questions to facilitate discussions and to help reach a deeper understanding of these leadership issues. Sit down with a peer, a mentor, or your significant other and see if they might, through truthful feedback, help take your leadership skills to another level. Don't be in a hurry. Take one chapter at a time and see where you are with respect to each of these leadership topics and how you and your team might want to make some adjustments.

Woven throughout each of these chapters are various leadership vignettes. They are taken from both military and business settings and represent opportunities to learn from good (and bad) leaders about the business of leaders. They are examples of the battle-tested strategies that are *Leader Business*.

Many leadership books attempt to define the difference between management and leadership. I think you need to be good at both, but I like author Stephen Covey's definition: "Management works in the system; leadership works on the system." Leaders are constantly seeking ways to improve systems that will make people successful. Legacy builders and difference makers know that change is constant. Everything can be improved. Good ideas are only that until leaders make them real. *Leader Business* takes a systems approach to this examination of leadership by suggesting points of leader input and new ways to see the roles and responsibilities of leaders as system engineers.

Note that the *Leader Business* model used in this book is circular; it has no defined start or end point. Each step is continuous and simultaneous with respect to the others. Effective leaders must understand that leadership is neither linear nor strictly by-the-book. They must be multi-dimensional, full-spectrum, multi-disciplinarians who are engaged in all elements of the cycle: always planning, preparing, executing, and learning. Just like the units at the NTC, our teams may be executing one project while we plan the next. Learning is continuous, with feedback that shapes both future plans and current operations. Leaders must be working in all areas, in all directions: adjusting systems, gaining victories, always moving forward.

Finally, it is worth noting the picture in the center of this model. This is what leadership is all about. Yes, the leader is at the top of the stairs, but her actions are focused down—on her people. This is the theme of *Leader Business*. It's not about how leaders plan, but how leaders provide input to help the team see the big picture, to make planners more effective. *Leader Business* is about preparing subordinates for success, helping them win, and making them successful. Leaders are not focused on themselves. It's not about us.

Now let's move out. Our troops are counting on us. Grab your rucksacks, mount your trusty steeds, and let's examine this business of leaders, beginning with the leader's role in planning and setting the conditions for success. This, after all, is *Leader Business*.

PART I

PLAN

Chapter 2

Leaders Plan

"A good plan, violently executed now,
is better than a perfect plan next week."
GENERAL GEORGE S. PATTON

Through a haze of fatigue and hunger, I heard the instructor bark out: "Ranger Jones, you're no longer the Patrol Leader. Ranger Magness, you're in charge now. Conduct an information exchange with Jones, determine what you are going to do, and get moving. You've got 15 minutes."

The scene was the middle of some godforsaken Florida swamp, in a night so dark you literally couldn't see your hand in front of your face. I'd just been following the guy in front of me, hoping I wouldn't get lost. Like my fellow Ranger students, I was cold and wet and wishing I was just about anywhere else. Unlike them, though, I was now the guy in charge . . .

I had no clue where we were or how far we were from our objective. I rubbed my eyes and tried to think of something inspiring to say, but nothing came to mind. The only thing I could think of was how far removed I must have looked from a leader you'd actually want to follow into battle.

But as I huddled under a poncho with my inner circle—four other tired, dirty and hungry Ranger students—and a red-lens flashlight and tried to formulate some kind of coherent plan, the training that had been hammered into us kicked in. It was a methodology I would rely on time and again: understand the purpose of the mission; assess the current situation; gather the facts; identify and evaluate alternatives; make a decision and issue guidance and instructions; and provide enough timely information to subordinate teams to plan and prepare for the mission. Within minutes, we knew what needed to be done and how responsibilities would be assigned.

How many times has this been you—in the middle of a major crisis at work, when the stuff really hits the fan, and thankful you aren't in charge? That was me . . . until they called my name!

Everywhere we look, the challenges associated with creating a roadmap for the team seem to hamstring the ability to execute the mission. A corporate CEO struggles to create and share a vision for her company. A non-profit executive director cannot align requirements with limited resources. A school principal fails to develop a long range calendar with holidays, teacher in-service days, and inclement weather contingencies. A state governor tries to ram through a budget without consensus and is surprised when all parties align against him. A unit manager becomes so risk averse that all creative energies within her team are suppressed.

Make no mistake: Planning is hard. It requires disciplined thought and analysis. It is rarely as glamorous or rewarding as being in the arena and actually executing those plans and strategies. And because it creates an audit trail that makes us accountable (our plans = our problems), it often makes us vulnerable to criticism.

Yet this is what we expect our leaders to do. Planning and decision making are among the key deliverables of those in charge. Who else can set the course for the team? Who else can decide among equally viable alternatives? Who else can inspire the team to take risks and is qualified to decide how much risk is appropriate? This is the unique domain of the man or woman in charge. Good leaders should be exercising this muscle every day, with repetition after repetition—making decisions, adjusting strategies, evaluating risk, and establishing and communicating a shared vision.

Unfortunately, most leaders lack basic planning skills . . . or are too timid to step forward and accept this particular responsibility. What we need are people—in our businesses, on our teams, and on our school boards and city councils—who are rooted in reality, with a depth of experience that can translate words into action and broad goals into focused objectives and executable tasks. We need risk takers, aggressive leaders who take bold but measured action, change-agents who see two or three moves ahead of everyone else.

How do we become those kind of leaders? Let's start with an analysis of planning and decision-making.

The House of Pain

The planning trends that I have observed during my diverse career are generally the same from unit to unit. You may recognize some of them yourself. Subordinate staffs lack guidance from their leader (the unit commander, in my case) to do what they need to do. Subordinate teams receive instructions late, which means they usually lack sufficient time to do their own planning. No one really knows what the boss wants; in fact, the consensus is that not even the boss really knows *what* he wants. Plans lack creativity; risks are neither identified nor mitigated; and there is no consensus on how best to actually execute the mission.

> *"Plans are only good intentions unless they immediately degenerate into hard work."*
>
> **Peter F. Drucker**

As a trainer at the NTC, we affectionately labeled the plans tent the "House of Pain." It was there that staffs dedicated countless mind-numbing hours to the development of operational schemes and orders. It was invariably too small for the number of people (all of whom had not bathed in a week!) who would cram in with charts and notebooks filled with data and analysis. The marathon planning sessions frequently started in the late afternoon and lasted until 0400 or so—what some of my peers called "oh-dark-hundred." I called it crazy!

Frustrations would inevitably peak when the unit commander, who had been noticeably absent during the all-night planning sessions, suddenly strode in and announced that the plan was not what he wanted—although what that was exactly was anyone's guess. The results were predictable: more delays, less sleep, and a growing assemblage of ticked off subordinates. Even if no one said a word, we all knew what we were thinking: "Where was this genius yesterday afternoon? We still have no clue what he wants, but we can be sure that what he just said is un-resourceable and un-executable. And now we'll have to spend the next six hours making a plan that is just as good (or as bad) as the one we've spent the last six hours preparing."

I hated the House of Pain! I hated the sleepless nights as an operations officer during my own training missions at the NTC. Even worse was the time I spent in there as a coach, where it was all I could do to resist pushing the training unit planners out of the way and doing it myself so we could all go to bed! But as painful as it was, the military's planning process was fundamentally a good one. Good plans and quality decisions are the product of three key factors:

1. A systematic evaluation of the problem

2. The identification and evaluation of alternatives

3. The issuance of guidance and instructions in a timely manner.

Others may teach something different or suggest an alternative approach within a time-constrained environment . . . but they would be wrong. This is the way to do it. Trust me—I've got the House of Pain battle scars to prove it!

Whether under the poncho or in the House of Pain, successful planning all comes down to leadership. Someone must be able to rise above the mud and provide a vision for what success looks like. They must be able to synthesize input from multiple sources, especially from those who will ultimately be responsible for implementing whatever plans are created. They must select a winning course of action, demonstrate an ability to mitigate risk to an acceptable level, and cultivate a desire to act with boldness and audacity. Leadership is the grease that overcomes the friction inherent in translating one person's intentions into the actions of others.

There have been very few sleepless nights with the red-lens flashlight in my assignments outside of tactical units. But there have been just as many challenges in strategic planning. In command assignments with the Army Corps of Engineers in Los Angeles and Detroit, it was just as critical that we had a systematic approach to developing appropriate goals and objectives. We had to strike the necessary balance between immediate requirements and long term needs. Billion dollar budgets needed to be adjusted to reflect our priorities, diverse, multi-million dollar, multi-stakeholder projects needed to be completed, current and future customers identified, and crises managed . . . or better yet, averted.

In each of my leadership assignments, I have embraced my role as "lead planner." I firmly believe that my use of battle-tested approaches for building winning plans has served as the impetus to reach ever-higher levels of organizational excellence. Just as I had done in combat operations, I worked with key leaders, conducted a detailed analysis of the mission, aligned resources, and drew a roadmap for our strategic future. I was able to provide my team with a clear vision, outlining where I wanted to be, what success would look like, and what my priorities were.

At the end of each of my tours of duty, I believe the accomplishments of my teams were a testimony to the power of strategic planning:

- At the Detroit District with the Army Corps of Engineers, we set in motion what later became a multi-billion dollar Great Lakes restoration initiative by bringing diverse stakeholders together and working hard to find consensus among them.

- At Fort Irwin, my team established a new Department of Defense training center to help defeat roadside bombs, literally wrote the book on how to assess infrastructure and utility issues in combat scenarios, and radically reorganized to meet a new mission requirement.

- In Los Angeles, again with the Army Corps, we doubled the size of our revenue, added a $200M business line focused on the Department of Veterans Affairs, completed over 220 miles of fence along the Mexican border, and transformed a team challenged with meeting milestones to one whose execution set the standard for this enormous federal agency.

In each assignment, I received top marks on my evaluations and was consistently recognized as the best officer among a very competitive group of highly qualified peers. But more importantly, the teams which I led were measurably better when I departed. The planning skills which I had learned under the poncho and in the "House of Pain" were validated as I became a more senior leader, albeit in drier and more restful settings!

> *"The time to take counsel of your fears is before you make an important battle decision. That's the time to listen to every fear you can imagine! When you have collected all the facts and fears and made your decision, turn off all your fears and go ahead!"*
>
> **General George S. Patton**

Planning is the critical first step in the *Leader Business* cycle. Without it, there is not even the *possibility* of success. The next three chapters will address the leader's roles and responsibilities when it comes to planning. It starts with the ability to see the big picture. We need "visioneers" who can see over the horizon and guide a team towards goals and objectives that achieve a higher purpose. The next step is helping the team develop coherent, focused strategies and tactics. Finally, leaders must know the value of boldness—how to take *measured* risks. The sum of all of this is the sort of aggressive, difference-making leadership that is the result of effective planning skills.

Leader Business

There are two extreme leadership examples we want to avoid with regard to planning. I saw them too frequently at the NTC and see them every day in business settings:

- *Eternal planners.* These are the colonels, CEOs, and agency heads who take so much time developing their plans, there is no time for subordinates to prepare to execute them. They will literally still be working on their plans while the problems they are trying to solve either compound or work themselves out. Slow, deliberate and detailed, these leaders consume all the time that could be spent on preparing and executing the mission, all in search of the *perfect* plan.

- *Micromanagers.* These well intended leaders eliminate all energy and initiative by telling everyone exactly what must be done and how to do it. There are limits. Again, these leaders consume time that could better be used for actually doing the work. Subordinates under these controlling leaders have no room to develop creative solutions to problems, as their every movement is dictated in the *perfect* plan.

Let me introduce the concept of *good enough* when it comes to planning. There are limits. It is important that we develop *reasonable* plans that have a chance to work and empower our teammates to determine the rest. Leaders do well when they focus on things like strategy, vision, and the resourcing of success. Turn people loose and give them enough guidance to get going. Figure out the rest in the arena! I have met leaders who are planners and cannot execute . . . and those who are poor planners but can fight their tails off. We need to be somewhere in the middle.

Planning is not a solo flight. Things like strategy, vision, and bold, hairy initiatives are not the singular responsibility of the leader. It is a team effort. The best ideas come up from the trenches. The visions with the greatest possibility of success are those which include the input from those who will implement them.

Good planning is an iterative process. New information causes us to reevaluate our facts and assumptions. New problems demand solutions consistent with our overall strategy—or new strategies to address them. Leaders must have a constant "running estimate" that continuously monitors strengths and weaknesses, looks for emerging markets, and assesses the competition. This running estimate is factored into our long-term strategies and day-to-day tactical plans and causes us to balance every piece of information against our current plan. Sometimes we adjust and sometimes we stay the course. But we never stop thinking about our plans . . . or making new ones.

Marching Orders

- *What is your vision for your organization? Who else knows this and what are you doing to make it a reality?*

- *Are the goals and objectives for your unit clearly defined and have they been shared with all who need to know?*

- *How do you generate alternatives and make decisions? How adequate are your current methods? How effective are your solutions?*

- *Would your subordinates describe you as a risk taker or as risk averse?*

- *Are your subordinates getting the guidance they need to generate their respective plans? Is it timely?*

Chapter 3

Vision Casting
(How to Hook the Really Big Fish)

"A genuine leader is not a searcher for consensus
but a molder of consensus."
MARTIN LUTHER KING, JR.

When President John F. Kennedy said that the United States would put a man on the moon, he said it with such power and conviction that he captured the imagination of an entire generation of aspiring astronauts. When Dr. King shared his dream, he changed a nation and inspired people everywhere to refuse to accept limitations based on physical characteristics. When Bill Gates looked into the future and saw a personal computer on every desk, he changed the way we communicate forever.

Have you ever served under a visionary leader, one who could see the future so clearly it was as if he had already been there? Do you know a leader who can describe her goals and dreams with such passion and commitment that you want to be part of that team? What about you? Are you a leader whose sense of strategic direction is capable of captivating the imagination of your entire team?

These qualities are in short supply—in our nation, our communities, and our businesses. True leaders with vision are few and far between. Too many leaders think tactically, in terms of immediate actions and short-term decisions, without any comprehension of the big picture. They lack an understanding of how all the actions and decisions will connect to accomplish something meaningful. Small thinking produces small results (and big problems down the road).

Big, hairy, audacious, visionary thinking produces big results and a bright future.

Don't be fooled by the fact that "the vision thing" has become the subject of work-place satire. I can think of no more important leadership responsibility than the development, sharing, and execution of organizational purpose and direction. This "vision thing" is the critical first step in planning: identifying where we are going. Regardless of the size of the company, the number of customers, or the composition of the workforce, nothing is more important than establishing the strategic direction of the team. Think of it this way: we don't get into our cars, trucks, or tanks and just take off without having a destination in mind. The "vision thing" is no joke; it's what people who are serious about leadership provide the teams they lead.

The best military leaders I worked with at the National Training Center (and in various settings before and since) were all very capable "visioneers." They each had the ability to project in time and space the relative positioning of subordinates and the machines they drive, fly, or launch onto the objective. I could watch them work out the complex calculus of questions such as: Where will my troops need to be positioned on the objective in relation to the enemy? Where will they be in relation to one another? How do I position my strengths against the enemy's weaknesses while protecting my own vulnerabilities? At even higher levels, strategic "visioneers" can see in dimensions that most of us cannot. They can predict second and third order impacts of their actions and they understand the people, processes, organizations, and equipment that are necessary to achieve these end states. They anticipate future adversaries and are already maneuvering to defeat them.

It may surprise you, but the most capable leaders with whom I have served have not been dictatorial, fire-eating types. Instead, they were masters at gathering input, building consensus, and arriving at a shared view of the future, one in which the entire unit was invested. Then they would relentlessly communicate that vision—with passion—until the full team was unified to achieve it.

So let's start our planning boot camp with the development of a shared vision. A good shared vision includes the following critical components:

- Identifies the destination. *Asks, "How does it end?"*

- Is ambitious while challenging and inspiring people to stretch. *Is bold, hairy, and audacious.*

- Articulates purpose. *Answers "why?" and "where?" in order to determine "what?"*

- Describes critical deliverables. *Identifies "key tasks."*

- Builds consensus through involvement. *Seeks "bottom-up" ideas and solutions.*

- Is well articulated, easily understood, and willingly embraced. *Is communicated relentlessly.*

How Does It End?

One of my favorite expressions describes the very essence of visioneering: "If you don't know where you are going, any road will take you there." The foundation of leadership is to know (or, usually more accurately, to figure out) where we are going so we can successfully identify the road that will take us there. Very often, this means we put less into steering our respective "ships" and more into determining the course and heading. It sounds paradoxical, but as leaders we have to begin . . . with the end in mind!

Too many leaders want to think small, jumping right into the nuts and bolts of each step of the journey. That's not only a waste of time, it's a potentially dangerous waste of time. Before thinking about "what" needs to be done and "how" to do it, we must first define "where" we are going and "why" it matters. We have to share

Developing a Shared Vision

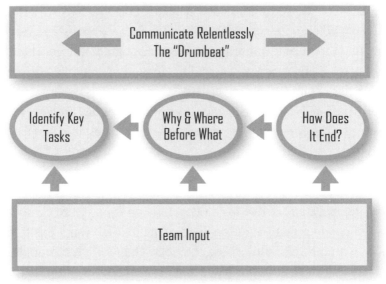

our vision for what it will look and feel like when we are standing on the objective with the mission accomplished:

- Why is it important that we change? What does this change look like?

- What unique niche will our organization fill in the world or in our community?

- What are the implications for our business lines? How will this benefit the organization in general and each of us in particular?

- Who are our projected customers, and what will we be doing to thrill them?

This sort of thinking does not come naturally—or easily—to

many of us. One proven approach is to invest in a formal analysis of the organization through a detailed assessment of SWOT: Strengths, Weaknesses, Opportunities, and Threats. A good SWOT analysis will help determine what the future holds for a company and its customers, current and future employees (demographics, generational norms, etc.), any competitors, and the overall operational climate in which the organization delivers its unique products or services. An appropriate end state is one which leverages strengths, protects weaknesses, seizes opportunities, and minimizes any possible threats.

In the military, defining the end state is the result of what we call *mission analysis*, a deliberate process to "see yourself, see the enemy, and see the terrain." Before a commander can give his planning guidance and define his strategic vision for a future campaign, he will conduct a deliberate analysis of the mission using this framework with his staff and trusted advisors. Only with a thorough understanding of both existing and future operating conditions (many of which are assumptions based on present understandings and good situational awareness) can the leader articulate his vision.

The mission analysis model that I learned in the military correlates very neatly with the more traditional SWOT and is the logical approach to determining the end state:

- *See Yourself.* Determine your strengths and weaknesses. What is your mission? What are you uniquely good at, and where are your holes? What are the demographics of your team, your customers, and the community in which you do business? What is your recent performance record?

- *See the Enemy.* Identify any threats to your operation. Who is your competition and what are they doing? What internal and external threats could pose problems to your business and its bottom line?

- *See the Terrain.* Look for opportunities and threats in the environment in which you do business. Where can you align your strengths with a need? Can you make money from it? What can you do to shape the terrain in order to gain an advantage over your competition?

Bold, Hairy, and Audacious

Too many leaders think small. If you are not passionate about big victories, I suppose this is OK. If you are not interested in inspiring people to hit home runs, then I suppose the small-ball approach will suffice. But if you want people to join you on the journey, to share in your vision, then you need to be able to challenge and inspire them.

I like author Jim Collins' use of "Big Hairy Audacious Goals," or BHAGS, as the end state that inspires people to make the leap from "good to great." We need leaders with the sort of vision that demonstrates courage, leaders who are able to map out an inspiring future, and leaders who are willing to accept the risks that come with bold action. I don't know about you, but that is the sort of future that gets me out of bed in the morning—both as a leader and as a follower. Like President Kennedy's commitment to put a man on the moon within a decade, capable "visioneers" must be willing and able to reach high and take on the big challenges.

"Why" and "Where" Before "What"

Teammates need to understand the purpose behind the vision. In other words, they must understand *where* we are leading them and *why* it matters before they even begin to determine what it is that they will need to do to get there. Leaders must be able to describe with clarity their view of the future. They must be able to articulate why change is necessary and the consequences to the team without it. They must be able to describe the reason for action and the good things that will happen when they are successful.

Purpose is the context in which the organizational vision makes sense and can be embraced by the entire team. Warren Buffet once remarked, "Someone's sitting in the shade today because someone planted a tree a long time ago." If we can articulate to our subordinates the need for shade and help them envision the wonderful benefits of a fully matured forest, we can launch an entire army of tree planters.

Think about the long-term, strategic future of your organization. What is the end state you envision? Why is it important that your team get there? Can you put this in terms that everyone can understand?

- *What is the impact on the company bottom line? What's in it for the work force?*

- *How will this make our operations and services better, cheaper, faster, safer, or more sustainable?*

- *What does this mean in terms of jobs?*

- *Why should people be excited about this envisioned future? And why is this any different from anything they've heard before?*

- *What sort of immediate, measurable accomplishments will we pursue to create irreversible momentum and help everyone understand where we are going?*

Identify Key Tasks

The difference between dreams and real vision is action. In my experience, there are too many "dreamers" and not enough true "visioneers." I like to think of it as putting some meat on the vision bone. Leaders must identify those critical enabling actions that will ensure progress toward the envisioned end state.

Consider the vision of Dr. Martin Luther King, Jr. His vision was more than just a dream. He identified key tasks, the achievement of which would make his dream a reality:

- Live out the true meaning of the creed, "We hold these truths to be self-evident, that all men are created equal."

- Transform attitudes so that "little black boys and black girls will be able to join hands with little white boys and white girls and walk together as sisters and brothers."

- Create a nation where children "will not be judged by the color of their skin, but by the content of their character."

The identification of key tasks sets a vision in motion. These critical goals and objectives provide credibility to the envisioned future by breaking the journey into smaller steps and tactical-level objectives. For example, they might describe the requirements for new products or services, and the necessary adjustments in organizational structure that will be needed to bring them to life. Similarly, they could define necessary performance measures and evaluation criteria, education and training standards, cultural adjustments, process changes, and a comprehensive communication plan.

> *"If you want to build a ship, don't herd people together to collect wood and don't assign them tasks and work, but rather teach them to long for the endless immensity of the sea."*
>
> **Antoine de Saint-Exupery**

In military settings, leaders identify intermediate objectives that must be accomplished or captured in order to reach the final goal. These key tasks could be the seizing of a significant piece of terrain from which to launch the main or supporting attacks, or the elimination of key enemy weapon systems that will enable ultimate victory. It could be a description of the level of risk that should be included in the final plan and the left/right limits in which any final tactics should fall. These intermediate objectives often serve as a roadmap to the envisioned end state and break the big picture into individual missions that can be assigned to subordinate units. Think of them as an articulation of the critical elements of the way ahead.

Similarly, I used key tasks to help my Army Corps teammates in Los Angeles see the way ahead on some big corporate goals. We wanted to be recognized as a regional center of excellence for coastal processes. In order to do so, we needed a different organizational structure. We needed to hire new skills and to establish a training and certification program worthy of that level of excellence. We needed to change our processes, seek out new customers, and publish a white paper about how we would operate in this new construct. Now if I had just said, "Let's become a center of excellence," people may have struggled to embrace it. But by identifying key supporting tasks, my team could begin to see the way forward. I wanted our shared vision to have enough detail for my teammates to say, "Yeah, I get it. We can do this!"

Visioneering From the Bottom Up

There is no debating the fact that we get the best "buy in" for our vision and strategic direction when subordinates are included in crafting them. It is also equally true that while the leader is ultimately responsible for steering the team and determining its direction, the best results will come from teams whose members are included in developing and shaping the plan.

Effective "visioneers" will solicit team input to shape the end state, focus the purpose, and to identify key tasks that will enable success. Through deliberate inclusion of as many people as possible, we can transform an organization, changing fellow dreamers into passionate co-owners of a shared vision.

At the Army's National Training Center, the most successful leaders were those who included the meaningful input of subordinate commanders. In my experience training hundreds of units and their leaders, execution was almost universally better from troopers and subordinate leaders who felt like their input counted. Additionally, "bottom up" plans and strategies were usually flat-out better than "top down" plans developed in a vacuum by commanders and their staffs who understood little about what worked down in the trenches.

The most successful "visioneers" with whom I have served often demonstrated skills similar to proven marketers. They were constantly soliciting input on the envisioned future, conducting informal surveys of subordinates on proposed courses of action, and working tirelessly to build consensus within the unit. They did so not because they were weak and indecisive but because they sincerely valued input, were humble enough to recognize that they didn't know everything, and understood that mission success requires "buy in" from the entire team. They were not seeking a vision around which the team could reach consensus, but rather to build consensus around the destination (first) and then the journey.

The fact is, most team members do not generally respond well to the top-down, majority-rule approach. Most, especially younger workers, generally appreciate a more consensus-oriented approach. The resulting vision produces two powerful characteristics within an organization: empowerment and ownership. Empowerment comes from teammates who feel like their input matters, who are involved in problem solving, and whose concerns are identified and addressed through the development of the shared vision. Ownership is the result of subordinates' readiness to embrace the solutions that they helped craft, ultimately leading to more efficient, effective, and timely execution.

Communicate Relentlessly

Once crafted, the vision should be a positive, inspiring story worth telling and retelling. The business of leaders is to be able to passionately articulate the road ahead in terms simple enough that every member of the team can embrace it . . . and retell it as if it was their own! Jack Welch, the legendary former CEO of General Electric, cautioned against using jargon and complicated "office-speak" in communicating a vision: "Targets cannot be so blurry they can't be hit." Use positive words with clear meanings and identify objectives that logically lead to the envisioned end state.

My good friend, retired Army General Randy Castro, was famous for wandering the halls and engaging people one-on-one about his vision. You could see the trail he left (and the impression he made) on sheets of butcher paper and dry erase boards throughout his headquarters. He used these sessions for several purposes: to refine his vision based on the feedback he received, to practice his delivery, and to win over converts—one person at a time. Remember, the process of communicating your vision often begins by sharing it with a few trusted advisors. Rather than "yes men," find people who will give focused criticism and honest feedback. If those people don't "feel it," perhaps it does not have the appeal you seek.

> *"No person will make a great business who wants to do it all himself or get all the credit."*
>
> **Andrew Carnegie**

Once you are ready to share your vision with larger groups, talk to your board of directors and get their feedback. Engage customers for their thoughts and ideas. Share your perspective of the future at every opportunity. Ensure it is a positive, inspiring story—one worthy of followership. Seize every opportunity to enlist others to help spread your message. Make each team member a co-owner of the way ahead. Continuously communicate the vision, path, and purpose until it becomes a *drumbeat* for the organization to march to as they move toward the objective. This is how you transform an organization and turn dreamers into fellow "visioneers." This is the essence of shared vision.

Leader Business

Bill Hybels, a visionary church leader near Chicago, subscribes to the theory that a vision should be concise enough to memorize. Print it on cards that employees carry with them. Put it on posters displayed in break areas. Send out emails with regular reminders of where you are headed. Record videos of team members talking about the vision or doing things that help people see the vision in action. Trust me—I've used all of these tactics, and they work. They are simple ways to remind your team that excellence is only possible through their combined efforts. Cheesy? Perhaps. Positive? Always.

Daily guidance and direction should be put in context within the framework of your overall vision. Each step you take must be in the direction of your intended end state. Every goal you achieve should reference those key tasks you identified as enablers of your vision. Things like performance counseling, metrics, new hires, bonuses, and equipment purchases must all be aligned with your strategic direction. Activities that do not make measurable progress toward your envisioned end state should be eliminated.

Our visions should have a definable timeline and clearly attainable goals and objectives. While Presidents may project out 10-20 years, most of us do not have that sort of foresight, nor the luxury of waiting that long. Too many leaders will project out into the future and stop. It's easy to do that sort of meaningless "thinking out loud" when you know you won't be around to see it. Anyone can be bold, hairy, and audacious when things are that far away—and we won't be held accountable for whether they come to fruition.

Instead, we need a clear, simple, executable vision that looks 1-3 years out. Most organizations simply cannot see further than that. We might have some idea of what the future could look like in 10-20 years, but we just cannot wait that long to transform the organizations we lead and achieve meaningful, measurable success. Frankly, it is difficult to maintain a drumbeat for that longer duration!

Sometimes we suffer from blurry vision and cannot see 1-3 *days* ahead, let alone the sort of future state described here. If that's the case, it may be time for some rest. We may need a vacation or even a sabbatical. We cannot allow the urgency of the present to inhibit our ability to project our thoughts into the future. If we don't, who will? In my experience, leaders who find themselves too busy to work on the "vision thing" will soon have plenty of time on their hands. No *employees* or *customers* . . . but plenty of *time*! Get enough rest to climb up to the top of the ship's mast and look beyond the horizon.

Regularly reflect on your vision and make adjustments as the situation requires; don't be too proud to make mid-course corrections if you determine they are needed. Review your accomplishments and strategic direction regularly with your teammates and remain open to new input. When you do, you will have a truly shared vision. More importantly, you will be ready to roll up your sleeves and start detailed mission planning, turning bold ideas into actionable assignments. You didn't think it ended here with vision, did you?

Marching Orders

- *What techniques can you adopt to help communicate your vision? Is the "drumbeat" of your vision loud and clear?*

- *Have you conducted an organizational SWOT analysis? Is it factored into your shared vision?*

- *How have you solicited input from your teammates to ensure that your vision is truly a **shared** vision?*

- *What "bold, hairy, and audacious" goals are you pursuing?*

Chapter 4

Plan to Win Or . . . Plan to Fail

"Take time to deliberate, but when the time for action
has arrived, stop thinking and go in."
NAPOLEON BONAPARTE

At 1200 hours one blistering Mojave Desert afternoon, I observed as a very capable commander whom I was training walked into his NTC field headquarters to receive an update on his unit's next major operation. His staff presented him with an analysis of the mission, outlined enemy strengths and weaknesses, identified friendly dispositions, and helped him visualize the urban terrain on which the proposed mission would be conducted.

It was good work by his subordinates. Before he departed to discuss this operation with his senior leaders, he issued enough guidance to shape the courses of action he wanted his staff to examine and the key considerations that he needed to ensure were included in the final plan.

At 2300, the commander was back to meet with his team. They laid out the details of each course of action they had investigated, highlighting the strengths and weaknesses and explaining the impact of each possible plan on friendly and enemy forces. He took a few minutes to visualize the end state of each course of action, "seeing" the relative positioning of his unit against the enemy and understanding the actions that must be accomplished by subordinate units to reach the ultimate objective. His staff continued by outlining the risks and mitigation measures for each alternative.

After careful consideration and several pointed questions, the commander approved the recommendation of his staff. It contained all the elements of the intentions that he had outlined in his initial guidance. He highlighted a few final details that he wanted included in the instructions to subordinate units, made a slight modification to the suggested risk mitigation steps, reviewed the timeline, and left the command post after asking his staff if they needed any further guidance. It was a "good enough" plan that, combined with the skilled "executers" in his formation, would add up to a bad day for the enemy. In a few hours the orders would be issued and the 4,000 soldiers of his brigade would begin movement, as one, toward the objective.

A recent study by the U.S. Army War College investigated critical behaviors of senior military leaders. Few skills ranked higher on the required attributes list than the ability to plan missions, solve problems and make decisions. In fact, the top four behaviors detailed in the study highlighted the importance of mission planning skills:

- Sees the big picture; provides context and perspective. (There's that "vision thing" again . . .)

- Clearly explains missions, standards, and priorities.

- Able to make tough, sound decisions on time.

- Keeps cool under pressure.

There's no way to sugar-coat it: leaders who fail to plan ultimately plan to fail. Whether developing long term goals or putting out the fires of day-to-day tactical operations, leaders must be equipped with an appropriate framework, a tool that systematizes the planning process. Combat leaders use a basic approach to mission planning called the Military Decision Making Process (MDMP). When followed, it produces the leadership behaviors that the Army has highlighted as priorities for senior leaders: timely decisions, big picture context, logical plans, and clear mission orders. The MDMP is a reasoned approach to identifying and evaluating potential courses of action before deciding what must be done. It can be used for planning major campaigns or for discrete missions and operations. This is the battle-tested methodology that enables quality decisions by calm decision makers.

What follows is a simple, four-step approach to mission planning, regardless of whether it is in a military or a business context. It's how we turn *vision* into *action* and strategic plans into tactical missions, tasks, and work assignments. It can form the foundation for the sound decision making and logical planning skills that we so desperately need from our leaders.

Step 1: Define the Problem

Mission planning cannot begin without a deliberate effort to define the problem. Thus, this step begins with a thorough understanding of the big picture and the operational context for the mission. Just as with the establishment of the broader vision, leaders must have good situational awareness and be able to "see themselves" (organizational capabilities, individual skills and strengths, and activities of other "friendly" units with potential impacts on the mission), "see the enemy" (competitor actions), and "see the terrain" (operational environment, future trends, customer demographics) for more discrete, tactical plans. This focused, mission-specific analysis becomes the base from which mission planning can begin.

Next, facts and assumptions that apply to the problem must be analyzed and understood. Quantify what is known and make logical conclusions about what is not. Good situational awareness (SA) about the operational environment will generally allow for assumed future conditions that are *good enough* to support decision making.

Problem definition must then identify requirements by addressing the following questions:

- *What tasks are specifically required to complete the mis-*

sion?

- *What tasks are not specifically required but are implied in order to reach the intended objective?*

- *Of these tasks, which are absolutely essential and must be highlighted as such in the final problem statement?*

As with facts and assumptions, write out this list of tasks and make a special designation for those tasks deemed as "essential." All of these tasks, whether specified or implied, must be assigned to some member of the team in order to successfully complete the mission.

Finally, restate the problem. Write out a mission statement that addresses the five "Ws": who, what, where, when, and why. Ensure it addresses all essential tasks. The restated mission should be posted throughout the problem-solving process to eliminate energy and time applied against the wrong problem—a common shortcoming in mission planning.

Following a detailed mission analysis and definition of the problem, leaders must provide their input. Issuing guidance any later in the process results in wasted time and frustrated subordinates. Leaders shape the problem solving process by clearly stating their *general* intentions for a solution. They identify what they are looking for in a viable course of action and those criteria (i.e. cost, speed, impact on customers, etc.) that have the greatest importance in the final evaluation. They must make known where they are willing to accept risk, and where they are not. The goal is to empower subordinates, to give them the freedom to develop creative solutions. Subordinates generally need only their left and right limits, if there are any. They'll figure out the rest.

While working with leaders at the NTC, mission planning could be an exasperating exercise. Frequently, commanders would share with me their frustration about plans that were not what they wanted or that they knew would not achieve their intentions. Unfortunately, they never shared their intentions with anyone else! They failed in this critical step and had not provided the guidance necessary to shape the final plans. They might have shared their vision, but never went into the level of detailed guidance that is necessary to produce plans that move the organization toward it. They left it to others to read their mind, a skill which unfortunately is not resident within most teams.

This is a task that cannot be skipped, or even delegated. Nor can the leader provide guidance later in the process. I have watched numerous subordinate staffs virtually implode after an all-night planning effort was destroyed by commanders who interjected their guidance long after the train had left the station. Not only was critical planning time lost; perhaps even more importantly, so was the staff's confidence in their leader.

Step 2: Develop Alternatives

In mission planning, leaders should attempt to identify at least three possible courses of action, all of which *must* be viable alternatives for solving the problem. Each course of action must meet the following criteria:

- *Is it feasible?* Don't waste time on alternatives that have no possibility of accomplishment.

- *Is it sufficient?* Does it address all the elements of the problem statement outlined above? A half-solution is no solution at all.

- *Does it meet the leader's intent?* If not, it cannot be considered as a viable alternative.

- *Is it bold?* At least one alternative should be audacious and blow through the boundaries of "business as usual."

Step 3: Analyze Alternatives

Once alternatives are identified, they should be deliberately analyzed and debated with respect to the relative strengths, weaknesses, and risks associated with each. Potential courses of action should be measured against critical evaluation criteria (again, those criteria that will differentiate one alternative from another, i.e. cost/speed of implementation, savings, risk, etc.). Criteria with greater relative importance should be weighted accordingly. This sort of deliberate analysis will help leaders compare apples to apples and enable selection of the most promising course of action.

> *"When you cannot make up your mind which of two evenly balanced courses of action you should take—choose the bolder."*
>
> **General William Joseph Slim**

Military leaders conduct a deliberate analysis of each proposed alternative. These are free-play exercises (war games) conducted on a map or in a computer modeling scenario that predict outcomes by looking at enemy actions and friendly reactions, much like a game of chess. These movements are carried all the way through the final objective with notes taken, casualties assessed, and relative positions recorded. This is an effective way to understand second and third order effects of proposed courses of action. While deliberate and somewhat time consuming, there is no substitute for seeing anticipated actions "play out" to enable an understanding of the strengths, weaknesses, and associated risks of a proposed alternative.

Step 4: Make a Decision

Ultimately, of course, leaders make decisions. That is what they get paid to do. After analyzing alternatives, it is the leader's role to select the preferred option. If the recommended solution is not adequate or does not meet the intent of the mission, it's time to modify it or, worst case, go back to the drawing board. And while clearly the leader's prerogative, exercise caution when rejecting recommendations from your team. You don't want to destroy the creativity and motivation of those subordinates to come up with bold, fresh ideas.

Once the alternative is selected, move out. Leave no doubt about the decision: "OK, here is what we are going to do." Issue *mission orders* and instructions to the entire team. Communicate tasks and purposes with guidance that is either specific (when specificity is required) or intentionally broad when subordinates have the latitude to work out the details on their own. Leaders must ensure that everyone is engaged, understands the big picture, and acknowledges their own mission requirements.

Note that I used the term *mission orders* above. In this approach, leaders provide the task and the purpose for the operation and all necessary resources. They tell people *what* to do. They do not tell them *how* to do it. That part is left to subordinate leaders and teammates. Mission orders result in maximum flexibility for solving problems and enable the sort of amazing initiative we all want to unleash in our teams.

Ranger School was a lot more than surviving for two months on no sleep and one meal per day. It was a small unit leadership laboratory that emphasized the value of clear, detailed mission orders. I have found that no matter the setting, people need enough guidance to get going and should be provided at least the following information when communicating decisions and plans:

Situation: Describes the big picture and the context for the mission.

Mission: Gives subordinates the "5 Ws," the most important of which—why?—provides the purpose and motivation for the mission.

Execution: Includes a description of the overall concept of the operation, along with specific tasks for completion and contingency activities based on friendly or enemy actions. *Mission orders* are used to give maximum flexibility to subordinate teams. Tasks, measurements, due dates, and roles and responsibilities are made clear to every element of the team.

Resources: Ensures that supplies and mission-essential resources are sufficient to accomplish the mission. Forecasted resource demands are a critical output from the war game/alternative analysis step and help leaders proactively address key logistics issues.

Command/Communications: Addresses critical communication issues pertinent for the mission, such as the location of the leader on the battlefield, as well as how and when important decisions will be shared across the team. This area also deals with the time and methods for follow-up and how team members will be held accountable to each other.

Plans and tactics that result from this process are likely to be well thought out and reasonable solutions. In other words: *good enough*. These plans will synchronize the activities and responsibilities of the entire team. Most importantly, this planning methodology should produce a consensus decision, crafted by subordinates who take ownership of that which they must ultimately execute. And because of the logic in this approach, each of these decisions is a step toward the ultimate goal described in the shared vision.

Planning In a Time-Constrained Environment

Many scenarios require immediate decisions and do not allow for such a deliberate planning process. In combat, leaders might be forced to grab a few key subordinates and huddle over a map spread out on the hood of a Humvee. Even in these instances, however, steps are not skipped—they are instead compressed to fit the time available. And by no means is a lack of time ever a justification for immoral or unethical decision making. The right thing is always the right thing, even when we have to make quick judgments.

The framework is the same. We still have to understand the problem, tell people what to do, and give them what they need to be successful. Wherever possible, include the input of one or two trusted agents, even in the most time-constrained situations. Our abbreviated planning process might be as simple as asking and answering these questions:

- *What's the problem?*

- *What are the available options, and what is the most important evaluation criteria?*

- *What is the best course of action?*

- *What are the possible second- and third-order effects of this alternative?*

- *What are the risks, and how might they be mitigated?*

Understand that this process is not supposed to be a rigid, lock-step approach but rather a framework for logical decision making. I've found that once people understand it, it can be easily adjusted based on the situation and the time available. I have used it to develop strategic plans for a billion-dollar organization as well as to solve urgent, life-and-death problems.

Great leaders are ultimately able to do this exercise in their head, especially in time-constrained situations. They are able to "see" relative future positions and anticipate second- and third-order effects as a way to shape decisions and anticipate outcomes. No doubt, it is an acquired skill, one that comes from the experience

> *"In any moment of decision the best thing you can do is the right thing, the next best thing is the wrong thing, and the worst thing you can do is nothing."*
>
> **Theodore Roosevelt**

gained through the more deliberate exercise. But I like to remind people: you have to first understand the deliberate approach *before* you can shorten it!

Now, a word to the wise: Leaders who consistently find themselves in time-constrained decision making situations would do well to examine the causes of these limitations. Deliberate planning helps leaders anticipate (and often eliminate) future problems and enables early positioning (both organizationally and individually) for future opportunities. Without it, we will be spending our energy perennially putting out fires. In other words, time-constrained decision making is all too often a self-inflicted wound!

Check Your Plan

While there is no such thing as a perfect plan, there are some important considerations to ensure the viability of your mission. The military has identified five operational tenets—depth, agility, versatility, initiative, and synchronization (D.A.V.I.S.)—that can be used as a leader checklist to gauge the potential success of current and future operations. These operational rules are battle-tested principles that reflect the combined wisdom of generations of military leaders.

1. Depth:

Successful plans demonstrate depth. This implies a vision of the "battlefield" and an understanding of the mission that extends beyond the immediate, to account for second- and third-order effects of each action. Unfortunately, most leaders do not look deep enough, do not see over the horizon, and do not develop plans aligned with the bigger vision of the organizations they lead. Depth in planning requires an allocation of resources that balances investments both for current and future requirements, looking across all the mission requirements.

Business plans create depth by broadening the customer base, seeking opportunities for growth or expansion in new areas. Similarly, depth suggests a diversity of products and services that will provide a hedge against difficult financial times or the loss of key customers. Finally, depth suggests that no element of a plan is reliant on one person, one machine, or one product. To be one-deep in any component of a plan is a recipe for disaster.

2. Agility:

Operational agility is the ability to react decisively through empowered subordinates without getting bogged down in layers of bureaucracy. Agility suggests plans and strategies that anticipate customer needs while responding faster than one's competition. It is achieved through teammates who see more clearly than the competition, often through the use of technology, proactive reporting, and shared information. Agile organizations are matrixed and lean, with teams not bound by burdensome processes and stovepipes. Subordinates are empowered to make decisions at low levels and people are given the resources they need to accomplish their respective missions.

3. Versatility:

Versatile plans are flexible, adaptable, and designed to meet diverse mission requirements. They are based around project-specific teams, tailored as required. Teams are equipped and staffed to take different forms and shapes based on customer needs and the organizational capacity to meet them. They are prepared to seize opportunities if and when they present themselves. Multi-functional team members are highly trained, with a variety of relevant competencies, and are able to move easily from project to project with speed and efficiency. Whereas agile plans allow us to respond to external conditions and rapidly change the way we approach the mission, versatility in our plans gives us the ability to flow from mission to mission without the need to stop and reorganize.

4. Initiative:

Initiative results from empowered teams who have the willingness and ability to take independent action. Plans and strategies must explicitly reflect the conditions for teammates to act independently and demonstrate creativity in problem solving. Allowances for initiative in plans help generate employee-owned "bottom up" solutions. In most cases, mission orders are the way to make this happen.

Initiative is unleashed when plans are developed within the framework of a shared vision. There is a direct relationship between the *ability* to take initiative and the degree to which subordinates understand—and buy into—the big picture.

Case in point: My good friend and West Point classmate, Nate Sassaman, was among the first Army battalion commanders in Iraq to hold elections and establish local government institutions following the initial invasion. While never directed to do so, he knew the future of Iraq, and the ultimate ability of U.S. forces to leave that country, was directly related to democracy and free elections. Nearly two years before national elections would do the same thing, Colonel Sassaman's initiative led to planting the seeds that would ultimately change history.

5. Synchronization:
Synchronization is reflected in plans with a logical arrangement of activities in time, space, and purpose. Leaders ensure that plans effectively synchronize personnel, resources, goals, workloads, and subordinate leader actions. They must clearly identify the decisive event or priority activity around which the organization must be synchronized, and plan, prepare, and execute accordingly.

In the "good old days" of analog combat training at the NTC (i.e. before digitization), I could look at a military battle map in any unit's field headquarters and find pushpins that represented friendly and enemy unit locations. My boss, then Army Colonel Rick Lynch, created the secret to synchronization: the Big Fat Tack (B.F.T.). He personally placed the enormous B.F.T. at the decisive point on the battle map. Staff members and subordinate commanders understood without question what was important, and the decisive events around which they would be required to synchronize their own actions.

I have used this technique with equal success in non-military settings. In my command in Detroit, Michigan, our B.F.T. was at the lock at Sault Ste. Marie, the northernmost part of Northern Michigan. It was our number one project and employed the greatest number of my people. In Los Angeles, it was along the border, where the construction of 225 miles of fence along the U.S.-Mexico border had Presidential visibility and a very tight timeline. Placing the B.F.T. at the decisive point (among hundreds of other important ones) within both of these organizations made my priorities clear to my staff. We regularly reviewed our collective alignment with respect to the B.F.T. When I moved the  "Big Fat Tack" to another location, I ensured everyone knew it, and we re-synchronized accordingly. It was a great visual enabler for organizational synchronization—and a highly effective tool to help keep our plans and operations focused on our priorities.

Leader Business

Leaders should engage in mission planning only for those problems and decisions that *must* be made at their level. If subordinates are empowered to solve problems and make certain decisions at their level—don't pull this authority back from them. Similarly, don't allow them to get lazy and push it back up to you!

Allocate an amount of time for mission planning that reflects the needs of the situation. Take all available time, but not one second more. If decisions must be made right away, make them. If not, allow the situation to develop, gather additional information, test your plan with those whom you trust, and wait. Don't be in a hurry to execute poor plans drawn up in haste.

Communicate your decisions and mission plans. Ask "who else needs to know?" Check higher, lower, left, and right. All mission plans must have a communication component that includes the workforce, customers, suppliers, shareholders, your boss, and anyone else impacted by your plans.

Never allow the urgency of the situation to create an excuse for taking short-cuts. Commit to plans that are morally sound, regardless of how others may justify the ethics of the moment. No personal or professional short term gain from a dishonorable decision is worth its long term cost—ever.

Marching Orders

* *Where is your B.F.T.? Have you done an analysis (like D.A.V.I.S) to ensure that your team is aligned with this decisive event?*

* *How do you generate alternatives and make decisions? How adequate are your current methods? How effective are your solutions?*

* *Would your subordinates describe you as a risk taker or as risk averse?*

* *Are your subordinates getting the guidance they need to generate their respective plans? Is it timely?*

Chapter 5

Be Bold, Think Big,
Take (Managed) Risks

*"Vision is not enough; it must be combined with venture. It is not
enough to stare up the steps; we must step up the stairs."*
VACLAV HAVEL

Upon assuming the role of coach/trainer at the NTC, I assembled my "get right on it list" for my team of 50. On it I recorded my initial assessment of gaps that needed to be filled, new initiatives that needed to be pursued, and short- and long-term priority projects that were consistent with my team's mission. I knew exactly where we needed to go. Mind you, we could have been content to simply do our jobs. Arguably that was difficult enough. But, I told my guys, we were on a different course. We needed to think bigger than that!

They called me the "good idea fairy." I'll assume it was a compliment. There was simply too much that we needed to do. Our "customers" (units preparing for deployment to combat zones around the world) deserved more from us. They deserved our best. Those good ideas would be stepping stones for my team to achieve our strategic plan. My intent was simple: be the best, keep moving forward, be bold, make a difference.

The results spoke for themselves: we completely reorganized our team, incorporating new specialties that reflected the Army's shift to modular organizations; we created a multi-million dollar center of excellence for roadside bomb prevention; and we developed tools to help engineers doing reconstruction work in Iraq. We hosted two worldwide training events, changed our team's internal operational procedures, and wrote and published a dozen professional journal articles. We expanded the roster of units that would train at the NTC and grew the menu of tasks to be trained—both of which were consistent with what we were seeing in Iraq and Afghanistan. And we did all of this on top of our "day jobs" as trainers.

That "get right on it list" (our strategic plan) became a guiding accountability document that propelled my team to another level. I used it (handwritten on coffee-stained scratch paper, believe it or not) when I sat down with my senior team members for staff meetings and for performance reviews. I kept it on the center of my desk and personally reviewed it at least once a week. Through the tireless efforts of my team, our bold intentions became realized actions. And by the end of my two-year assignment as "Sidewinder 07," we had accomplished more than I suspect any of us would have thought possible at the outset.

Everyone makes plans. We all have capital plans, business plans, career development plans, even vacation plans. Some are good. Some are barely worth the paper they are printed on. But very few include the sort of bold risk taking that gets people out of bed in the morning. In fact, most plans are designed to stay within the status quo rather than to challenge it. BOR-ING!

Consider, for a moment, the risk takers in business and in life. These are the game-changers, the ones who lay it on the line, personally and professionally. In business, think of Steve Jobs, Henry Ford, or Fred Smith. In politics, consider Dr. Martin Luther King, Jr. or Ronald Reagan. In the world of sports and entertainment, look at Jackie Robinson or director James Cameron. They are the risk takers, the first to embrace their fears, to carefully measure the risks, and to take bold action. More than simply "visioneers," each of these great men embodies the leader's ability to manage risk in a way that unleashes the potential for greatness in both themselves and their fellow citizens.

Risk is inherent in everything we do: business lines dry up, suppliers miss delivery deadlines, and people misinterpret what we ask from them. For those in leadership positions, the decisions we make every day can cost people their jobs, their retirement savings, or—especially in the Army—their lives. But with great risk comes great reward. And if we want to make people excited to follow us (for the most part, "followership" is a voluntary endeavor), we need to find ways to generate bold ideas and initiatives in our planning while ensuring that the inherent risks are minimized to the greatest extent practicable.

In the military, every mission we plan is loaded with high risk: heavy equipment, night operations, lack of sleep, enemy action. There are very few low risk operations. But the leader's job is to manage the risk to an acceptable level in order to facilitate safe mission execution. His or her job is to know the unknown—*before* the competition can figure it out and *before* it can present conditions that can harm the team or jeopardize the mission. It is a continuous assessment process that is conducted at all echelons, and one that can definitely help you sleep more soundly at night.

So let's finish this section on the responsibilities of the leader by putting squarely on his shoulders the responsibility to first think big, to go after the "high-hanging fruit;" and second, to identify and minimize the risks in doing so. Maybe I'm in the minority here, but for me, this is what makes leadership fun: pushing myself and others hard, making people successful, achieving excellence. There's no hand-wringing allowed out there "on the edge." It's lonely out there. But man, does it make life worth living!

Think and Act Boldly

In 2007, college football's Boise State Broncos played the heavily favored Oklahoma Sooners in the Fiesta Bowl. Oklahoma had everything going for it: size, speed, experience, and roster depth. Perhaps they did not measure up in one critical area: heart. It is there that the passion for winning and the willingness to lay it all on the line in pursuit of bold, hairy goals is usually found.

As the game approached the final minutes, BSU trailed by seven points. They had fought hard, kept it close, but always appeared to be outmatched by the talent-rich OU squad. Yet, they never gave up and scored a touchdown with seconds to go. The safe play would then have been to kick the extra point and go into overtime. Instead, they went for two points, scoring on a wild "Statue of Liberty" play, one that is almost never used and rarely works, and won the game. Had the play failed, they would have lost. Instead, the coaches and players went for it all and won. Little Boise State defeated the mighty OU Sooners. That is bold, hairy, and audacious.

Boldness in planning means thinking differently. It means going beyond safe choices and pursuing radically new alternatives. The final determination of whether plans are bold or bland comes down to the person in charge. When we play it close to our vest, so will our team. When we really open up the throttle, we enter a whole different realm of possibility. Here's some advice about how to foster that culture of boldness:

- **Listen to your team.** The biggest, boldest ideas generally come up from the trenches. It can be a little humbling to admit that we are not the source for every good idea, but true leadership is about getting results, not taking credit. Remove the restraints from your team and challenge them to truly think differently, and you might be surprised by what they come up with. I am finding that more and more, when challenged to think "outside the box," many of our teammates didn't even know there *was* a box. Too often we're the ones as leaders who put them inside one with arbitrary rules and nonsensical policies and procedures. Empower your team to come up with ideas and listen to what they say. I promise you that they will raise the bar every time.

- **Challenge the status quo.** Leaders must ask whether the plan simply adheres to the status quo. If so, challenge it! Too often our plans have self-imposed limits that are the result of too-rigid policies or faulty assumptions. The best leaders I know aren't afraid to ask "Why?" and "Who says?"

- **Always evaluate at least one "out of the box" alternative.** As mentioned previously, when developing plans and strategies, ensure one option is *waaay* out there. You know, something like:
  - *How can we put a personal computer on every desk?*
  - *Why don't we find a way to guarantee delivery of packages overnight?*
  - *What if we did a movie completely in Aramaic, or in 3D, or in black and white?*
  - *"Mr. Gorbachev, tear down this wall!"*
  - *What if we significantly increased our troop strength and pushed them down into the towns and villages to truly help the populace understand our desire for peace?*

- **Have regular discussions about new and emerging opportunities.** Engage your teammates about bold, new options at every staff meeting and strategic planning session. Talk about emerging markets, new customers, and game-changing technologies. Don't be afraid. Keep every option on the table while exploring new ways to solve old problems. And don't let anyone squash a good idea as too risky. It just *might* work, remember!

Conduct Risk Management

Now that you have developed bold plans, you need a process to ensure that you are prepared when things don't go exactly as intended. (In the military we say, "The enemy gets a vote.") Risk management is both a formal part of the planning process and an intuitive, continuous "running estimate" that is part of the leader's every consideration and contemplation. Its basis is a formal assessment process that must be both personally and collectively reviewed in order to

avoid surprises, to account for worst-case scenarios, and to mitigate the potential impact of damaging operational conditions. Here are the basics:

- **Identify potential risks.** Begin your assessment by identifying any significant concerns with your plans and operations. We cannot establish a culture of risk-taking without first identifying that which could go wrong. Conduct a "what if" analysis to determine the potential risks. What operational conditions could get someone physically hurt? What changes in the business climate (economic uncertainty, competitor actions, shifts in the customer base, supply-chain interruptions, etc.) could harm the organization? What fears stand between the team and the accomplishment of our big ideas?

  Measure each area of risk as a function of the probability of occurrence (high, medium, low) and the potential impact to the team (catastrophic, negligible, etc.). Assess each as a function of the possible impact on mission, personnel, equipment, loss of product or income, or impact on the environment.

- **Identify risk mitigation measures.** In most cases, risk is never completely eliminated—it is instead managed or mitigated to a more acceptable level. Leaders must take the time to evaluate solutions that minimize either the probability of occurrence or the severity of the outcomes. Be specific and consider each risk with clear, focused solutions to lessen potential impacts. It might look something like this:

  - *Risk: Injury during construction or use of tools and equipment. **Mitigation:** Training, safety equipment, insurance, etc.*

  - *Risk: Disruption of supply chain. **Mitigation:** Pursue other vendors or consider different material solutions.*

  - *Risk: Loss of major customer. **Mitigation:** Focused customer management ("care and feeding") while seeking opportunities to diversify the customer base.*

  - *Risk: Major project failure. **Mitigation:** Detailed communication plan, emergency response contingencies, and business lines that can offset any projected losses.*

- **Assess your residual risk.** Once all the potential risks are identified, assessed, and mitigated, some risks will still remain. Unless we are playing it close to the vest and wrapping everyone in bubble wrap, some things can still go wrong. This residual risk should be analyzed for any lingering concerns. Is it acceptable? If yes, execute your risk management plan and take off toward your bold goals. If no, consider additional means to lessen the risk. If the residual risk continues to be high, leaders can choose one of several options: accept the risk and take a chance (not recommended); identify additional mitigation measures to bring the risk to a more acceptable level; or pursue additional, less risky courses of action.

As a general rule, leaders should be wary of considering any course of action or operating conditions with risk that cannot be mitigated below "High Risk," ones with high probability of failure and possibly catastrophic consequences. I have found that there are ways to mitigate almost every risk. Occasionally, the cost to do so may end up eliminating some of those high risk alternatives from consideration. Then again, those mitigation steps may give you enough confidence to take off in pursuit of the big prizes.

- **Supervise and Evaluate.** It always comes down to leadership. Ensure you have appropriate control measures built into the plan both to monitor execution and to make certain that specified mitigation measures are in place. Clearly assign responsibilities for both—never leave anything to chance. Instead, provide training to ensure that subordinate leaders are prepared to execute required mitigation measures.

Finally, identify metrics that serve as early indicators of problems. There are usually data points that, when monitored, are clear predictions of a project "going south." Ensure subordinates understand the importance of observing and reporting this information—it may allow you to "pull the plug" before an event becomes truly catastrophic.

For instance, military units position dedicated observers such as scouts or other reconnaissance platforms to get early warning of worst-case scenarios. For high risk operations, military leaders will position trusted subordinates or even be present themselves to help ensure safe and successful execution. Business organizations are no different. Metrics are identified to get early indicators of problems.

Key leaders are personally positioned to meet with no-fail customers or to watch for threats to the plan.

My assignments with the Army Corps of Engineers had us on constant alert for possible disaster response events. In Los Angeles, believe it or not, the most likely situation was a flood response. We had a detailed risk management plan in place. We conducted training and rehearsed the most likely and most dangerous scenarios. We identified early triggers based on forecasts and upstream gauge readings that would allow us to respond. Finally, we positioned key leaders at various disaster response headquarters to facilitate coordination and our own people at possible points of failure in the system to give us immediate reports on flood readings. We did the best we could to mitigate the potentially catastrophic event down to something we could manage.

> *"Only those who will risk going too far can possibly find out how far one can go."*
>
> ***T.S. Eliot***

Leader Business

Leaders should never confuse risk taking with gambling. The former is the domain of bold leaders who have established proven means of protecting themselves and their teammates. The latter is for dummies! What's at stake is nothing less than the potential health and well-being of your organization, your employees and their families, your customers, your shareholders, and your own personal and professional survival.

It has been said that luck is the intersection of opportunity and preparation. Gamblers hope for good luck. French scientist Louis Pasteur, on the other hand, once said that "chance favors only the prepared mind." Risk takers meet every prospect head-on. Not only are they prepared for those narrow windows of opportunity, but they see them coming. Risk management is the process that enables leaders, through both deliberate analysis and continuous assessment, to make their own opportunities notwithstanding the occasional setback or *seemingly* unforeseen event.

Nothing stymies organizational growth like a culture of risk aversion. Subordinates must have a passion for success that far exceeds their fear of failure. Reward risk takers. Seek opportunities to recognize those who take on the biggest challenges and successfully navigate the most difficult hazards. Highlighting the accomplishments of those who are willing to climb the mountain (even with the threat of showing their tails!) will reinforce to the entire team your willingness to accept and manage risk.

Make the risk management process a focus of training—don't just assume subordinates will understand a system that you have not shared with them. Lead by example in this area and conduct regular risk assessments for critical events and major decisions. Ask to see your subordinates' risk assessments during site visits and project inspections.

Routinely end meetings with a couple of simple questions: "Where is our greatest risk right now?" and "Are we reaching high enough?" Then spend time with your team assessing any necessary mitigation measures. Nothing models risk management like a leader who assesses his vulnerabilities while still being unafraid to push the envelope in a routine, measured way.

Risk management should not be an afterthought to a finalized plan, but rather something that helps shape the entire planning process. It is also not a process designed to create fear, but rather one that clarifies an uncertain future and embraces that which often prevents the fulfillment of our potential. Teams and their leaders who identify what *could* go wrong, who implement steps to prevent such an occurrence, and who set in motion measures that minimize damage if and when failure occurs, are empowered to think—and act—boldly.

Marching Orders

- *Can you identify one bold idea that you are now pursuing? If not, why not?*

- *Are you reaching high enough? What would you do if you weren't afraid?*

- *Where are your greatest risks—personally, professionally, and organizationally? How are you managing them?*

PART II

PREPARE

Chapter 6

Leaders Prepare

"If good luck is what happens when preparation meets opportunity, bad luck is what happens when lack of preparation meets a challenge."
Darrell K. Royal

As a student at the Army Ranger School, I had to receive a "Go" in a leadership position in each of the four phases of the course: the woods at Fort Benning, the mountains of North Georgia, the swamps of Florida, and the deserts of Utah. In each phase, I was evaluated by both my Ranger instructors and my peers—a true 360-degree leadership evaluation.

It was in my role as Patrol Leader (PL) that I learned the importance of preparation and what it really took to translate *good enough* plans into winning tactics. After assigning tasks to the members of my patrol (using a clear mission order that focused on *what* each member of the team needed to do and *why*), it became my responsibility to stay engaged and ensure that my team was prepared for battle.

My collection of individual Rangers—all hungry, sore and exhausted—had to be formed into effective teams with specific assignments. Those teams then had to be synchronized to be able to operate together as a team of teams. In what was usually just a few hours (between issuing the order and executing our tasks), we needed to practice our roles, assign specific responsibilities, distribute resources, prepare ourselves, and be ready to jump out of a plane, traverse a swamp, or do whatever else it might take to reach our objective and accomplish the mission. No time for sleep—we had work to do!

As the leader, it was my responsibility to ensure that my fellow Ranger candidates knew their roles and were in sync with each other. They needed sufficient water, ammunition, and food (well, scratch that—they only needed water and ammo) in accordance with their respective assignments. My task as PL was to ensure that the conditions were set to make the execution of the plan possible.

Time was tight, by design. There was too much to do and not nearly enough time to do it before we packed up our rucksacks and began the mission. It was an environment in which I clearly learned the importance of time management, delegation of duties, empowerment of team members, and prioritization of tasks. In this constrained setting, I learned how to balance my time between many competing demands: checking on my men and verifying that each of them understood the plan, conducting inspections on key equipment, leading and participating in rehearsals that confirmed the suitability of the plan and the readiness of those who would execute it. I was also forced to continually ask myself about our readiness: What adjustments would I need to make to the plan? Were my men ready? What decisions would I need to make and what information would I need to make them?

It was quite the learning environment. We weren't always successful in our missions (it was training, thankfully). But I learned that *good enough* plans needed more work to be effective. Good preparations—both for me and those I led—filled in the gaps of the plan and ensured that my team of highly motivated Rangers would be ready to step across the line of departure and begin the mission. Good preparations gave us the *opportunity* for success.

So far in these pages, we've covered the basics for developing an inspiring vision for our troopers. We've learned how to ensure that it is totally and completely embraced by them all, largely because many of them provided input that helped shape its final form. We have learned how to develop *good enough* plans using mission orders that rely on the initiative and creativity of our energetic and motivated staff. Now it's time for the real work to begin. As I had to do with my Ranger Patrol, let's prepare ourselves—and those we lead—to accomplish the mission!

"Success is a ladder you cannot climb with your hands in your pocket," says one of my favorite old proverbs. *Good enough* plans are just the first rung on the ladder of success. To take the next critical steps, we have to remove our hands from our pockets, roll up our sleeves, and start the difficult, grinding work that generally occupies most leaders' time. I'll give you fair warning: this next set of leadership responsibilities isn't as sexy as "visioneering," and it doesn't come with a lot of glory or public accolades. But it is definitely *leader business*.

As important as planning is, it takes real leadership to translate those plans, goals, and dreams into actual achievements. The leadership duties within the *Preparation* phase are nothing less than the critical people-centric elements of our management responsibilities. Employees are hired and teams are formed, synchronized

> *"The men who succeed are the efficient few. They are the few who have the ambition and will power to develop themselves."*
>
> **Herbert N. Casson**

around a coherent mission, with tasks that leverage each person's unique strengths. New people must be brought on board, and new skills must be acquired through training and mentorship. Resources must be prioritized and aligned against requirements. Team members must be empowered to take action and be ready to execute the mission.

They gain this through practice and consistent, focused feedback on the behaviors they exhibit (the *how's*) and their alignment with the *what's* and *why's* that we have assigned them. These *preparation* tasks may not be the first things we think of when we think about the business of leaders, but trust me when I tell you that they will occupy the majority of our time!

Plan ▸ **Prepare** ▸ Execute

I like to compete as much as anyone. I like the excitement and the energy of being in the arena, of achieving greatness, and of gaining increasingly higher levels of individual and team success. If it was up to me, I would be perfectly content spending all my days outside at the construction site or providing the services for which my organization is known. Let's just get out there and start . . . doing stuff.

Unfortunately, it is just not that easy. *Good enough* in our planning means there is still work to do. Those strategic plans and tactical tasks are not ready for execution until the leader makes them so! Thus we see *preparation* nestled between *planning* and *execution* in our model.

As the CEO/commander of my Army Corps of Engineers unit in Los Angeles, I had the awesome responsibility of leading a great team with over a billion dollars in annual revenue. Our program consisted of hundreds of individual projects—some in the planning phase, some in design, and some in construction. We issued thousands of permits for development, operated and maintained dams and reservoirs, and responded to natural disasters. We had thousands of customers and millions of people who depended on us to do our job (nearly one out of every 10 Americans resided within our area of responsibility). It was an extraordinarily diverse mission and a wonderful area to work (if one can call it that!). I was blessed to have this assignment.

One could easily argue that just doing my job, executing this huge, diverse program, would have been enough. Well, either I have a restless streak or, more likely, I knew that would *not* be enough. We needed a plan that would make us *more* efficient, *improve* our customer and employee satisfaction, and *reduce* operating expenses. We had to identify organizational and individual employee improvements that would help us meet current and future customer requirements. We needed a strategic plan which would reflect all of this, one which would propel us forward *while* we executed our mission.

But as my team and I recognized, the plan itself was just a fancy document consisting of a multitude of goals and objectives—merely step one in our journey. The hard work of translating the goals and objectives in our strategic plan into reality required *preparation*:

1. Build the Team.

We needed to hire new employees with relevant abilities and proven problem-solving skills. Some people had to be dismissed if they no longer fit. Our existing workforce of over 800 highly energetic and motivated people needed additional training to get to the level of professional competence that our operations demanded. We had to organize differently for the ever-changing requirements. New teams had to be formed and new processes had to be put in place that would enable success. We had to investigate what concerns our customers had and put action plans in place to address them. Finally, if our plan was going to work, we needed to ensure that we had mechanisms to hold each other accountable: metrics, milestones, and forums to review our progress.

As with each of my previous assignments and command responsibilities, I found that there was a direct relationship between the collective readiness of my employees, the strength of our products and services, and the overall health of our organization. My team was made up of diverse *individuals* who needed to understand how much I valued every one of them. I needed each of them to have the requisite skills and tools to pursue both our *team* goals and their own personal ambitions. It begins with people, formed into teams of teams, ready to accomplish the mission.

2. Align Resources With the Mission.

In an environment of limited budgets (and with a strategic goal of reducing operating and overhead costs), decisions had to be made on the allocation of equipment, facilities, and funds. We had to clearly identify priorities and then align our resources accordingly.

Preparing my team meant ensuring that they had the necessary tools, equipment, facilities, money, and support to do their jobs. We clearly had more to do than we had hours in the day, so our priorities had to be clear, our metrics focused, and we certainly had to be disciplined about that most precious resource: our time.

3. Empower People to Act.

In an organization as large and diverse as the one I led in Los Angeles, I could not possibly be involved in every project or make every decision. I wanted people to take ownership in the plan and unleash their own creativities in solving problems and making changes.

> *"All the so-called 'secrets of success' will not work unless you do."*
>
> **Anonymous**

I wanted empowered employees to take on this mission. I wanted them focused on *how* to make things happen while I took on those broader strategic issues that would shape our uncertain future (the *why* and *what* of our mission).

Did it work? Well, I'll let you judge. In three years of focusing on preparing people to be ready, willing, and able to accomplish the mission, we achieved the following:

- Annual revenues increased from $400M to $1B.

- Customer satisfaction improved by 15%.

- Employee satisfaction improved by 10%.

- Overhead costs were decreased by 20%.

- Mission accomplishment within our major programs went from below 80% to 100%.

- We increased our workforce by 25%, added new business lines such as a new partner with a $250M construction program, and brought new life to some aging facilities. All in all, not a bad run!

Prep for Combat

In my leadership journey as a military officer, I have learned that these preparatory tasks are critical enablers of success. I have affirmed the notion that planning is not an end-state, but rather the beginning of the heavy lifting that ultimately determines success.

Good leaders lead disciplined organizations that do these routine preparatory tasks—routinely. They prepare themselves and the teams that they lead for battle. They ensure that information is passed, tasks are resourced, and events are rehearsed. They value their time and that of others. They build and sustain teams and take care of people such that they can accomplish great things. These are the critical leader tasks that occur after the issuance of orders and before execution that make victory possible.

At the NTC, my team of trainers had made it a science to quickly evaluate a unit's readiness for the mission. We had a proven methodology to build a snapshot on how effectively the warriors we were training had prepared for the tasks in their plan and whether the mission had any realistic chance for success. In general, we assessed the following issues. See if the specific areas we assessed point to a recurring theme:

1. Build the Team. Has the unit issued adequate guidance, flexible enough to adjust to any number of possible outcomes, through reasonable plans with reasonable expectations for success? Has that plan been issued down to the lowest levels? Does the plan assemble the necessary team of teams required for the mission? Has the unit considered appropriate risk management measures, and are those suggested controls being implemented prior to initiation of the mission? (In other words, most of the leadership elements we addressed in Part I.) Are leaders taking care of their people and ensuring they have what they need for battle? Are they confirming the alignment of subordinate tasks with the overall vision and mission of the team?

2. Align Resources with the Mission. Does the unit have the resources (fuel, ammunition, repair parts) in place to execute this mission? Has it been issued critical supplies and support consistent with its intended goals and objectives? Has the unit made good use of its available time? Do leaders work efficiently such that maximum time is afforded to subordinates for preparation tasks such as rehearsals and inspections?

3. Empower People to Act. Does the plan include adequate control measures to keep the unit within boundaries while allowing initiative at all levels to accomplish their assignments? Are the leaders circulating around and inspecting each of their troopers and their equipment prior to mission execution? Do all team members understand their roles and responsibilities within the context of the overall mission? Has the unit conducted practice drills at all levels to properly synchronize the pending mission and give people confidence in their ability to succeed?

These were the predictors of success that we used in training. Collectively these factors addressed leader responsibilities in preparing an organization for combat. They would not *guarantee* an outcome . . . but they came darn close. Units who got low scores on these metrics would generally not be able to "turn it on" during execution. On the contrary, leaders who invested in the oversight of these vital preparatory tasks were ready for battle—and usually victorious.

Leaders Prepare

I enjoy sports, especially at the college level. While I don't usually root for Duke in sports, I am always impressed with how its basketball coach (and fellow West Point graduate) Mike Krzyzewski gets the most from his team. While they are not often individually the most talented, they always play well as a team. Their NCAA championship in 2010 is another testimony to this fact. Think about the key elements of building a champion. These are the critical steps for preparation of any successful team . . . in any arena:

- *Recruit* the best players by embracing them as part of a family and demonstrating to them that they matter and that they can be part of something important.

- *Develop* individual skills and put the right person, with the right skills and tools, in position to succeed; assemble the team and get them to play together.

- *Synchronize* individual actions within each play and as part of an overall game plan.

- *Practice* hard and prepare for game situations, cultivating empowered teammates who thrive under the pressure of big games and can react faster than the competition.

As the Army slogan (*Mission first; people always*) suggests, success always begins with people. My own experiences in both the military and business operations have certainly validated this concept. Successful mission preparation begins with successful *people* preparation. People must be given enough guidance to be effective, yet not so much as to stifle their own initiative. They must be

"The men who succeed are the efficient few. They are the few who have the ambition and willpower to develop themselves."

Herbert N. Casson

formed into a team and resourced, rehearsed, and trained until ready to accomplish their assigned tasks. Thus, Part II of *Leader Business* examines the preparation of people—each with their unique combination of skills, strengths, weaknesses, dreams, and aspirations—in ways that enable the success of the mission. Leaders recognize that if they take care of their people, their people will take care of the rest.

The first steps in leadership—to inspire others, develop goals and objectives, and establish a road map for success—gets us out the door. Now the journey (and the sweat) begins.

Leader Business

Preparation focuses on ensuring that we have a mastery of the fundamentals. In the Army, leaders who are sound in doctrine, who have a solid understanding of basic battlefield "science," are much more capable of reacting in combat with quality battlefield "art." We have to understand the business. This is what most training produces—a common reference point from which decisions can be made and shifts can occur. Even in a tough economy, we must continue to invest in training people and growing future leaders.

Preparation includes taking the time to think. Whether in isolation or with a mentor, leadership coach, or peers whose ideas can stimulate thought, leaders must take time for themselves. This is where problems are solved. This is often where bold visions are birthed. This is the necessary recharging that gives leaders the energy they need to go the distance. In the end, we have to practice what we preach and do for ourselves what we insist upon for those we lead. We have to prepare ourselves.

Effective leaders get everyone in the fight. They focus every team member on the mission. I have found value in routinely going through the organization and assessing whether everyone is focused on mission accomplishment (remember the B.F.T.?) and the execution of essential tasks. Leaders are charged with creating an environment where subordinates believe (because you show them) that no one is any more or less important than anyone else. Subordinates who believe that their input counts, and that they matter to the mission and to their leaders, will fight to not let their teammates down.

There is probably nothing more destructive and less helpful when it comes to *preparation* than to abuse people's time. If we want them to have a chance to train, to think, to develop solutions, to determine the "how" for their respective missions, and to execute their assignments, we have to be respectful of their time. Long, pointless meetings or delays in sharing information that might enable effective mission preparation and execution are the sorts of "time abuse" that prevent people from doing what we want. Leaders who are focused on preparing their team give people the resources they need to be successful—the most important of which is time.

Author John Maxwell says that subordinates will not care what we know until they know that we care. Our preparations must reflect this theme of taking care of people. Effective leadership ultimately comes down to the relationship between the leader and her followers. Success is enabled through teammates that know that we care about them.

Victory in battle—whether in sports, military or business—is the result of leaders who are engaged in all elements of a "good enough" plan and preparing a well resourced, empowered, talented team of teams. *Planning* and *preparation* are joined at the hip. When we invest in fundamental leader responsibilities during this critical preparation phase, good plans become great ones. Good individuals form great teams. And great teams, like the Army Rangers, the training units at the NTC, Duke basketball, and the awesome team I served with in Los Angeles, are given the opportunity to achieve excellence.

Marching Orders

*   *Do you understand what it takes to translate "good enough" plans into winning strategies?*

*   *Are resources such as people, skills, logistics, and money aligned with the mission?*

*   *Are you building capable teams of teams to accomplish all assigned tasks?*

*   *Do you have a culture of "Mission first; people always?" Are you taking care of your "troops" and giving them the opportunity to succeed?*

Chapter 7

Jerseys Don't Make a Team

"Players win games, teams win championships."
BILL TAYLOR

A few years ago, using lessons learned from the early actions in Iraq, the U.S. Army formed a new combat organization within its fighting brigades: the Special Troops Battalion (STB). Created by joining signal, intelligence, engineer, military police, and other specialized units under a common headquarters, this unit's leaders faced a daunting set of tasks: build a team of teams out of these relative strangers; combine these dissimilar units into a cohesive, fighting organization; and accomplish the mission by making each of the individual units better than when they operated independently.

I watched as many of these units, some of which I had the responsibility of training at the NTC, struggled to come together as a team. They had good people and were very capable independent groups, but had a very difficult time working together and becoming more than just a collection of disparate functions. Their leaders did their planning, issued orders and instructions, but were unable to adequately prepare the team to successfully accomplish their respective missions.

One otherwise very capable lieutenant colonel with whom I was working was particularly challenged by this new reality. Having taken command of his battalion only a few months earlier, he thought his unit was coming together quite nicely. Unfortunately, I had gained a completely different picture from my team of trainers. To the contrary, we were seeing individuals and teams of teams who had nothing to do with each other. I felt like I needed to do an intervention and introduce the senior staff to one another. (Think of a business parallel in which the sales team doesn't connect with marketing, or a city in which the fire department has no relationship with the police or utilities department. Can you say . . . dysfunctional?)

After a few mission failures, I approached the struggling commander to get his take on the unit's performance.

"What's the problem?" I asked.

"I believed we were better than this," he responded. "I thought we were coming together."

"Do you really think so?" I asked. "What have you done to make your team into a functional, fighting unit? How have you prepared your troopers to work together as a team?"

"Well, we had a formal military ball last month and everyone really seemed to enjoy that. We developed a new motto that I thought we all liked, and I had it printed on our challenge coins. It sure seemed like we were connecting. I'm not sure what else I can do."

And then it occurred to me: the jersey does not make the team. The merging of people and their unique skills around a common purpose requires much more than just issuing plans and strategies (and much more than slogans and morale-building events). Teams of teams will not form themselves. That's the leader's job. Leaders are uniquely responsible for building the team, taking care of their people, getting them to work together, and sustaining high levels of excellence. Like good orders and instructions, jerseys get the team onto the field, but they won't be competitive until they are fully prepared.

Create Synergy

None of the preparation tasks we talked about in the previous chapter are new. They are what we are accustomed to hearing about in terms of leadership deliverables: hire good people, give them the skills and tools they need to be successful, form teams aligned against the mission, and take care of people and their families. But these efforts really just ensure that our people have a jersey, that it fits, and that the right players get on the field in the right position. There's no guarantee of success.

Unfortunately, that's where most leaders stop. The real mark of a successful leader, however, is the ability to transform individual players into championship teams. Doing so requires an understanding of the importance of the difference-making concept of *synergy*.

> *"Synergy is the increase in performance of the combined firm over what the two firms are already expected or required to accomplish as independent firms."*
>
> **Mark L. Sirower**

Are you familiar with this term? For non-engineers, it can be defined like this: *the whole is **made greater** than the sum of the parts.* Mind you, I'm an engineer, so I like to think of synergy in mathematical terms: $1+1+1>3$. In everyday terms, though, it means that people working together are capable of doing much, much more than they could do separately. And not surprisingly, the business of leaders is found in the action verb (*made* greater) that enables this seemingly unrealistic equation.

Successful organizations function as a team of teams. Organizing in accordance with the orders and instructions brings separate, independent units together for a specific purpose. Functions in existing operations are combined to streamline processes and harvest efficiencies. Business units are grouped together to leverage capabilities that may not exist without each other.

Only leadership will make this work. It is the grease that eliminates the friction inherent in team building. It is the forcing function that ensures the team of teams is, in fact, better than its former condition—more efficient, higher productivity, greater access to customers, and a better product—and that good individuals can work together as a great team.

My experience as a leader is that putting a group of good performers together under one roof does not guarantee synergistic success. They have to be *made better*. Think of how many companies have failed following a big merger or acquisition. Remember AOL + TimeWarner? Ouch! How frequently do we see mergers that yield no results and companies whose family tree can only be described as dysfunctional? Bigger is *not* better. Better is better!

There are four key steps for achieving synergy and making the seemingly impossible (1+1+1>3) a reality.

1. Common Vision, Common Goals

Leaders must create the common purpose for which the team will fight—together. Groups, no matter how mature, must have a reason for working together that makes sense to all team members. Without a shared vision and a mutual purpose and direction, organizations tend to form stovepipes, build up barriers, and focus on themselves. Synergy comes from teams and team members who are truly committed to working together.

Leaders provide the vision of how great the team can be when they are working together toward something significant. As is always the case with "the vision thing," leaders must believe it themselves and then share it (frequently and with passion, aka the "drumbeat"), first with internal customers and then with everyone else. Every member of the team must buy into the big picture and recognize the importance of the overall mission—and especially the vision and goals that will enable mission success.

2. BIG TEAM, little me

Synergy is created when team members subordinate their personal or small unit goals to those of the larger team. They must have the belief and understanding that they are successful only if the team is successful. The old way of doing business must be replaced with a new way—better and fully integrated into the higher organization.

The emphasis must be on team goals, not individual performance. Team rewards help identify the benefits of working together.

Behaviors that demonstrate the desired corporate mindset are highlighted so that people see what right looks like.

Leaders have to find the appropriate balance between the need to work as a team while still sustaining the competitiveness that drives subordinate teams to do their best. Sales teams push each other to achieve monthly goals while the top prize is reserved for when the company achieves its intended profitability—a measurement that involves the entire team, not just sales. In schools, teachers strive for individual recognition as good teachers, yet take the greatest satisfaction in their school's "exemplary" status (and are rewarded accordingly).

Synergy is achieved when teammates who strive to be their individual best strive equally hard to make each other better. Streamlined processes and cost savings are realized by team members who look outside themselves to help others. Information and new lessons are shared. The whole is greater than the sum of the parts.

3. Interdependence
Synergy is only made possible through team members who replace independence with the newness of interdependence. Organizations whose members are mutually dependent on each other's unique skills, experiences, and capabilities are more inclined to work together toward a common, higher goal. They are also less inclined to grow in size and scope, yielding higher levels of productivity and organizational efficiency. Instead of automatically adding another person, skill, or layer, interdependence forces us to seek unused capacity elsewhere within the team.

The Department of Defense continues to work hard to force its services to embrace interdependence, a concept known as "jointness." Does the artillery need a new howitzer when aviation—Army, Navy, or Air Force—can service those same targets with existing weapon systems? Does the Army need more bomb disposal personnel when the Navy has world class capabilities available to do this mission? A difficult concept with high stakes, interdependence is the only way to get the most out of a military force with as many commitments as ours.

My experience with the Army Corps of Engineers yields more examples of a large government organization wrestling with the need to create interdependence. Our budgets no longer allowed each regional organization to create fiefdoms known as "districts" with full functionality and whose sole focus was internal: district goals and district customers. Instead, regional and national centers of expertise were created to serve each Army Corps district. While in Los Angeles, my military design support came from the district in Sacramento. We relied on all the districts in our region to provide assistance in a variety of functions when our annual revenues shot up from $400M to $1B. Our business processes had to be modified to reflect the elimination of stovepipes and local behavior and the execution of our mission through a much more networked organization. Not only did interdependence make better business sense, it produced a better product and led to a more satisfied customer. I learned there in LA that it was possible to do more with less. That's synergy.

Good leaders prepare their teams by developing interdependent units who share everything: resources, customers, skills, people, and facilities. They identify unused capacity and determine how it can be applied to help the team. They cross-level resources and capabilities between subordinate teams to meet higher level goals. They build bridges and bonds between mutually dependent sub-organizations that create results that exceed what could be done individually. This is how organizations are *made greater* than the sum of its parts.

4. Accountability

Synergy is only realized when the team is literally, measurably, actually *made greater*. The parts must function together to make a better product—cheaper, faster, more sustainable, more reliable, safer. True synergy must result in increased revenue or larger market share. Economies of scale must be realized. Customers, both internal and external, must see progress.

Teams do well what a leader measures. Effective *preparation* includes the development of metrics for the team and for each subordinate organization that can be used for mutual accountability. Leaders create an environment where subordinates are free to "look outside their cubicles" while holding each other accountable for meaningful, quantifiable advancement.

Remember the Special Troops Battalion? Those leaders had the challenge of integrating diverse organizations, each with their own unique, specialized role, into a functional team. Synergy was realized when the Military Police commander could look across the table at the Engineer commander, two units who typically had nothing to do with each other, and question various performance metrics, asking how they could help them improve. This measure of accountability and interdependence did not exist in the former organization. The STB team of teams, to be effective, had to recognize that despite how effectively individual units may have performed their battlefield functions, when any one of them failed, the entire team failed. On the flip side, the soldiers had to discover that together, the whole could be so much more powerful than the parts.

Team members must be accountable to one another to ensure a better team. This is only possible when they understand each other and appreciate how they each uniquely contribute to the accomplishment of team goals. Education programs, such as new employee orientation and formal and informal professional development, help build employees who understand the broader team of teams. Peer reviews provide perspectives on subordinates who work well within the team concept. Best practices are shared across functional areas, making each component of the whole better than if it were operating separately.

Subordinates who understand that their success is only enabled by the success of every team member will begin to think outside themselves to help, and hold accountable, others. Salesmen will give constructive feedback to manufacturing partners. Marketers will interact with operations folks like never before. Peers and subordinate organizations that formerly had little interaction will develop productive, mutually beneficial relationships. This is a team prepared for the mission—and one whose performance will be better than the sum of individual talents and deliverables.

Accountability on teams is strengthened by the use and encouragement of "accountability partners." Matrix organizations and flat project teams need the support that comes from a dedicated partner. Independent operators are often ineffective without a sounding board for new ideas and a peer to help work through challenges and sticking points. Everyone, even a senior executive, needs someone to tell it straight and to keep them honest.

The U.S. Army Ranger School is famous for its buddy teams. My own Ranger School "buddy" never left my side during 60 miserable days in jungle, mountain, and desert training. We fought together, encouraged each other, kept each other awake, and maintained vigilance against the perils of heat, cold, hunger, injury, and the cadre of instructors that were looking for excuses to kick us out of the course. Even in the high performing U.S. Army Rangers, mission accomplishment is only possible through the accountability that results from these dedicated buddy teams.

Long-Term Synergy

Great teams make winning routine. Like many of the enduring Fortune 500 Companies (Wal-Mart, Ford Motor Company, General Electric, and AT&T are always near the top) or champion sports teams (think Duke basketball or the New England Patriots in football) with records of sustained excellence, great teams are built on fundamentals, usually without many superstars, but with role players who embrace the concept of *team*. They

> *"The executives who ignited the transformations from good to great did not first figure out where to drive the bus and then get people to take it there. No, they first got the right people on the bus (and the wrong people off the bus) and then figured out where to drive it."*
>
> ***Jim Collins***

demonstrate solid performance quarter after quarter, game after game. New players are added, products and services evolve, yet they just keep winning. Leaders must deliberately invest the time and energy necessary to sustain greatness.

Truly great teams embody a culture where no one on the team is irreplaceable. Subordinate leaders are capable of stepping up into positions of increasing responsibility, especially those who are included in developing the shared vision. Lessons are distributed across the team to further develop junior leaders and empower them to take action.

Our role as leaders is to ensure that we are never in a position where the loss of one team member due to illness, promotion, or a transition outside the organization will compromise the organization's ability to reach its objectives. We have to build "bench depth" across the entire organization. Forcing subordinates to take time off allows junior leaders the opportunity to "step up." This sort of empowerment makes employees feel like they really are part of the *big team*. Even more powerful is when we take time off ourselves and trust others to do what we have trained—and empowered—them to do. Remember: no one is irreplaceable, not even us!

Truly powerful teams demonstrate the sort of long-term synergy that comes when we provide incentives for effective *team* performance. If we want teamwork, we have to measure it, reward it, and model it through things such as:

- Focusing rewards on *team* performance (and having the courage to *not* give rewards when milestones are not met or corporate behavior is not demonstrated).

- Acknowledging the great accomplishments of our teams and team members, formally and informally, in public gatherings and during private discussions.

- Including the concept of "plays well with others" in performance reviews.

- Conducting 360-degree peer reviews to gain insights from team members that might not otherwise be apparent to leaders and using this input in our performance reviews.

Even winning teams have their disagreements and arguments. Team members must feel free to speak their minds and to offer opinions that differ from our own. Again, every voice counts. Teammates must feel like their contribution matters. Leaders have to make a choice to not only allow but to encourage dissent. As difficult as this often is to swallow, it helps with buy-in and provides the forum to hold us all accountable!

I've had success with this stated philosophy: *Until we make a final decision, every opinion counts. Personal attacks will never be tolerated. Arguments are acceptable. Professional disagreements are encouraged. Challenge everything. Speak your mind. Once we make a decision, then let's all agree to execute . . . as if it were our own idea. Until that point, let's have a family discussion!*

Sustaining winning teams requires an atmosphere that works and plays hard. Remember, we want to *keep* the talented leaders we have endeavored so tirelessly to hire and develop. Leaders must continually ask themselves if they would want to be part of their own team if they were not in charge. Let off some steam. Be creative. Use off-site meetings to stimulate different ways of looking at problems and further reinforce the belief in the team. Have fun.

One high level Army commander of mine would routinely blast the wildest country music he could find from the speakers in his tactical command post. We'd be in the middle of a stressful, late-night planning session when he would turn to one of the enlisted soldiers, give him the sign, and we'd all be singing along to a Hank Williams song. To an outsider, it might have seemed inappropriate to mix loud music with the discipline of tactical military operations. To those of us on the team, however, it was part of our unique "Raider" brand! This was synergy at its finest: a true team of teams. Quirky . . . but effective!

Leader Business

While jerseys do not a team make, leaders must be aware of the need to build a unique brand around their team of teams. Cross-training and developmental assignments between organizations help foster a better understanding of new acquisitions or within subordinate units who otherwise might not have reason to interact. Celebrate team accomplishments and organizational progress toward the common vision.

Money may be enough to get people to *meet* the standard. But more than compensation and benefits, people are motivated to *exceed* the standard, to achieve greatness, by human factors such as relationships, respect, fulfillment, pride. No better example of this is seen then in the United States Marines, where pay and benefits never enter into the equation.

Since 1883, the Marine Corps motto, "Semper Fidelis (Always Faithful)," has rallied men and women to a higher purpose. Semper Fi signifies the dedication, loyalty, and pride that Marines have to their organization (the Corps) and to each other: "Once a Marine, always a Marine." Semper Fi represents the belief in something bigger than themselves and the faith in the principles, values, and leadership of the Corps.

People want to know that their input matters. They want to be inspired, to make a difference, to see their work output add up to something meaningful. Leaders who care for subordinates see to it that each and every team member understands and is recognized for their unique, irreplaceable contribution to the team. They endeavor to create pride in the team and its product. They sustain relationships among teammates who must be willing to "do battle" together—for each other and for the team.

Synergy is fueled by communication and cross-talk. Economies of scale, opportunities for cross-promotion, and a better use of shared resources will not generally identify themselves. Leaders must constantly "wire brush" the organization to bring these issues to the surface. Constant dialogue about best practices and lessons learned, coupled with teammates held accountable to one another, will drive growth across the board. The total can exceed the sum of the parts—many times over.

There are many good teams but only a few truly great ones. Great teams are led by empowering, visionary, inspiring leaders. These great warriors understand that it is the leader's job to create synergy, to add value, and to make the team of teams *better* than its parts would be if they operated independently. Preparing a team to think and operate this way does not occur on its own. That's the business of leaders.

Marching Orders

* *What can you do to turn your collection of individuals into a team with a shared vision and common goals?*

* *How does your team hold each other accountable? Who is your accountability partner?*

* *How can you force interdependence among your subordinate teams and business units?*

* *What are you doing to prepare your team to think TEAM before SELF, MISSION before ME?*

Chapter 8

Leader as Chief Alignment Officer

*"Don't say you don't have enough time. You have exactly
the same number of hours per day that were given to Helen Keller,
Pasteur, Michelangelo, Mother Teresa, Leonardo Da Vinci,
Thomas Jefferson, and Albert Einstein."*

H. JACKSON BROWN

L eadership was a mandatory part of the West Point education. We participated in training and drills each summer. We
marched in parades during the week and on football Satur-
days. And we took a full slate of classes that focused on the purpose
and objectives of leadership, from military history to philosophy to
basic and advanced leadership instruction.

I am sure I only picked up a fraction of what the instructors
taught us. It was a bit overwhelming learning about leadership in the
early 80s from officers who had seen up close the difficulties of leading during the Vietnam War. Some of their stories made me question
whether I'd ever be ready. But most days, it was all I could do to stay
awake. I was, after all, only a cadet and a long way from ever feeling
the thrill of organizing teams and taking on big challenges.

What I do remember was probably the very first lesson I learned
in my very first class, something that has shaped my thinking about
leadership ever since. We talked about the responsibilities of the
leader, and our professor boiled them down to three things:

1. *Accomplishment of the mission.* (No doubt that this is, and
   always will be, number one.)

2. *Welfare of subordinates.* (This is the "people piece" of our business.)

3. *Efficient use of resources.* (Ah, the topic of this chapter.)

This third responsibility is a key component of preparing men and women to accomplish their respective missions. We have to align resources against requirements and make the best use of what we have. We need to equip people for success, make adjustments when priorities shift, and think about sustainability. Without accounting for item #3 here, we can forget about #1 and #2.

Meet the Chief Alignment Officer

Sometimes humor helps us learn about leadership in ways that more traditional teaching cannot. That may explain my fascination with the TV sitcom, *The Office*. Sometimes it is helpful to examine what *not* to do in order to ponder what we *should* do. Michael Scott, the show's main character and self-proclaimed "World's Best Boss," regularly champions his "big picture, visionary leadership," while discounting the importance of the day-to-day management of his office.

I can't tell you the number of times that this sort of non-alignment has baffled and befuddled me! I have seen countless examples of leaders who provide the vision but never identify priorities, never allocate resources, steal all of our time, and then wait at the finish line wondering why things don't turn out the way they had hoped. This is what happens when you jump directly from planning to execution, skipping the *preparation* phase!

So allow me to introduce the key role of the leader as "Chief Alignment Officer." This is where we connect the big picture with the reality of daily, direct action. This is where we determine priorities and ensure that those most important tasks and functions have everything they need to be completed. It is in this capacity that we ensure that everyone embraces the connection between ends (vision and strategies), ways (the details of how things will get done), and means (what people need to be successful). This is the heart of strategic leadership and key to effective *preparation.*

President Franklin Roosevelt provided an excellent example of the leader as Chief Alignment Officer. He masterfully communicated a shared vision for the defeat of Japan and Germany and the successful outcomes that would result from a coalition of freedom-loving countries waging war against tyranny.

The end goal was clear. The means to achieve it were equally well defined. FDR served as the nation's chief executive, promoting policies and legislation that would mobilize the nation and protect the United States and her allies against future attacks. He served as commander-in-chief for a military whose campaigns in Africa, Europe, and the Far East would ultimately achieve the desired end state. He crafted strategic alliances between the United States and international partners. Within the construct of total war, he ensured that the nation's tasks were consistent with its vision.

In his role as Chief Alignment Officer, FDR ensured that the means to be successful, the resources necessary to fight and win, were not neglected. Under his leadership, the U.S. mobilized millions of fighting men and women, adjusted the industrial base in order to equip the force, and developed a budget consistent with fighting a world war.

> *"Strategy without tactics is the slowest route to victory. Tactics without strategy is the noise before defeat."*
>
> **Sun Tzu**

Also key to the alignment of the nation was President Roosevelt's role as communicator-in-chief. His "fireside chats" ensured that the nation was prepared for sacrifice and had the necessary will to win. He dialogued regularly with national and international leaders, with his cabinet, and with the military warriors who would ultimately accomplish the missions, ensuring that the vision was clear, that the strategies were appropriate, and that the resources were sufficient for success. No matter the setting, his message was consistent (again, the "drumbeat") and the unifying thread that tied together the ends, ways, and means. Chief executive, commander- and communicator-in-chief—FDR embodied all of this in his role as Chief Alignment Officer.

Non-Alignment

In Los Angeles, I struggled to create the execution-focused organization that I envisioned. No matter how much I shared my vision, we couldn't seem to get to where we needed to be.

Then I checked our alignment. I had not resourced those critical team members who make project delivery possible: project managers. We were under-manned by probably 40%, meaning our existing PMs, the nominal leaders of the team, were swamped. The PMs we did have were lacking the basic skills to do their jobs. No surprise, with all the projects they had to manage, they could never find time to go to training! Moreover, we didn't even put our best PMs on our most important projects; worse, we weren't even identifying which of the hundreds of projects we had were most important. Despite my efforts, we had major alignment issues.

I take some comfort in knowing I am not alone in this area. Think of the alignment issues that have challenged our 43rd and 44th Presidents:

- Throughout his term, George W. Bush struggled to mobilize the nation to address the difficulties of the war on terror. The resources, whether in manpower or funds, were never reflective of what should have been a national priority. And to a fault, his message was certainly not as clear and consistent as FDR's. Major alignment issues.

- Barrack Obama has been challenged with aligning resources with his stated priority: jobs. Health care, foreign policy, an oil spill in the Gulf, wars in Iraq and Afghanistan, and day-to-day politics all siphon off energy from what people expected to be the focus of his administration. For a variety of reasons, some controllable and others not, the alignment of funds, messages, people and actions all have displayed, at various times in his tenure, a lack of consistency with his stated main concern. Again . . . alignment issues.

So you see, I am in good company! The key is to recognize the non-alignment, which I believe I did with great success with my Army Corps teammates in LA. We put our resources into recruiting and training our PMs. We had no choice given our increase in revenues from $400M to over $1B. We needed team captains capable of delivering on these higher demands. When we set our team, starting at the top, we began to overcome the alignment issues that challenged us.

Aligning the Means

Means are the resources necessary to accomplish the mission. In preparing people to be successful, we need to ensure that they have adequate skills and tools to accomplish their assigned tasks. Leaders provide the coaching, training, and mentorship to develop people capable of accomplishing the mission. They get the right person, with the requisite abilities, at the right place and time to do their absolute best.

People need adequate facilities, equipment, and support to do what they need to do. They need processes and procedures. They need to be armed with information and the full resources of the organization to be able to seize opportunities and function within the overall purpose and intent of the mission.

In most scenarios, and in most organizations, resources are limited. There is only so much one can do in terms of training, capital improvements, or new IT equipment. Usually, we have to prioritize and allocate accordingly. Leaders must be prepared to make the "tough call" based on an assessment of both short and long term requirements, evaluating the skills and tools required now . . . and over the horizon.

Remember our previous discussion about the B.F.T. (Big Fat Tack)? This notion of organizational priority is the basis for making decisions on limited resources. All projects are not equal. All initiatives are not the same. And all people are not necessarily on a level playing field. Making the hard call means allocating resources according to those priorities. This includes focusing meetings, refining metrics, and aligning the entire team with that priority . . . and being willing and able to explain why not everyone is number one.

A major component of the leader's alignment responsibilities is aligning the message. What we do and what we say must be the same. Priorities must be clear to everyone. Leaders must dedicate time and energy to the "drumbeat," helping people understand ends, ways, and means and how they connect. For the most part, everything a leader says and does should be aligned. Every speech, every presentation, and every opportunity to share ideas should be consistent with the shared vision and should help people understand how their combined efforts help the organization get there.

One final point on aligning our resources: alignment is not for short-term thinkers. The notion of *sustainability* (meeting the needs of the present without compromising the ability to meet the needs of the future) demands that leaders ensure that resources are available both for current requirements as well as future ones. The preparation of people and their mission requirements must look over the horizon, setting things in motion so they are ready when needed. Initiatives like sustainable design and construction standards, renewable energy, and recycling help ensure that the means for future success will continue to be available.

Align Your Watch!

Perhaps no resource requires more alignment than our time. There is always more to do than time will allow. In constrained environments, leaders must ensure that they and their subordinates have adequate time to plan, to prepare themselves and their own units, and to execute the mission. They must balance competing demands, build in periods for rest and learning, and make the most of every available minute.

In my experience, military leaders learn early that skillful management of their personal time increases their combat effectiveness, keeping them razor sharp and alert during extended periods of high stress and the demands of combat. More importantly, when they implement measures to enable the effective time management of the entire team, they set the conditions for sustained battlefield success.

Combat leaders who fail to manage their own time live an unbalanced life of high stress, continuous crisis, poor decisions, and personal disappointment. But those who cannot manage the time of the organizations they lead find that the mismanagement of this critical resource is a major source of anger and frustration with the troops and a principal cause of mission failure.

Our workplaces are loaded with leaders who simply cannot master time. Projects are routinely delivered late or incomplete. Short-term successes are offset by unplanned, long-term mission failures. Every day is another crisis, another round of "urgent" tasks, and another series of poorly synchronized activities. Workdays are painfully long and usually largely unproductive.

I call these leaders "time thieves." Despite the best input and coaching money can buy from time management books, articles, gadgets, and gurus, we still see far too many leaders like this. Subordinates who work for these people generally lack time for planning, rehearsals, inspections, synchronization, and personal and professional development—all the enablers of successful mission execution. The leader's poor clock management skills result in a downward spiral that ultimately hinders everyone.

Time is a finite resource. How we align, manage, prioritize, and allocate it—for ourselves and for our team—may be the best predictor of personal and professional health and sustained organizational success.

Time Management for Leaders

There are any number of publications that chronicle useful techniques to align time with requirements. These procedures can certainly help people prepare and enable better, faster, more efficient delivery of products and services. A good list of proven tactics might include the following:

- Use checklists and to-do lists.

- Come in early or stay late. Find a quiet time to get things done.

- Have a clear purpose and agenda for each meeting.

- Start and end meetings on time. Establish a clear suspense for each action. Identify minimum essential attendees.

- When possible, eliminate meetings!

- Don't answer the phone. Call back at a time of *your* choosing.

- Handle correspondence once. Use short responses and write quick notes.

- Throw away (or file) unneeded material.

- Maintain an accurate, shared calendar. Find a good tool and stick with it . . . until it no longer serves you. Then throw it away and get something better.

- Learn to say "No!"

These procedures, however, are only likely to make us incrementally more productive. These are just time management "blocking and tackling" drills. What is still required is an examination of the deeper alignment issues associated with time management.

Put First Things First

Aligning time, as with all other resources, begins with the establishment of priorities and following them. Leaders have to be disciplined enough to do what is critical first. They must invest in determining personal and organizational priorities, and ensure that scheduled activities are consistent with these requirements.

While serving a fellowship at the University of Texas, I had the chance to spend a morning with Temple-Inland CEO Kenny Jastrow. Temple-Inland is a diverse company that includes real estate holdings, timber, and paper products. Mr. Jastrow shared with me how he began each morning with an examination of his company's daily financial snapshot. He examined income, expenditures, specific metrics from each subordinate business unit, progress towards goals, and key events at the beginning of each business day. What better way to prepare for the day than by putting your finger on the pulse of your organization?

> *"If you want to make good use of your time, you've got to know what's most important and then give it all you've got."*
>
> **Lee Iacocca**

New York City mayor Rudy Giuliani began each day with his famous "morning meeting." He reviewed activities and performance measures with senior staff to create accountability and follow-through. Goals were assessed. Calendars were synchronized. Important events were reviewed and future plans were adjusted. Every work day began with a clear understanding of current status and future operations.

I tried to apply these lessons running my own billion-dollar operation with the Army Corps of Engineers. I started each week with a review of the calendar, a meeting with my executive staff, a look at our financials, HR statistics, and hot projects, and a huddle with my top leaders. I wanted to review our "Common Operational Picture," in conjunction with my senior staff, including our most pressing priorities, initiatives, and issues. These Monday huddles were the basis for our actions the rest of the week. I used them to check the alignment of my team, ensuring that their priorities were synchronized with our overall purpose and mission.

Putting first things first is equally important in our personal lives. How we manage our personal time impacts everything else we do. People watch to see if what we say ("Family is #1") is consistent with what we do (i.e. working late and missing key family activities). Consider what is important and what our failure to prioritize may be causing us to neglect: family, health, spiritual fitness. How can we reorganize our activities to ensure that these critical issues reflect our stated priorities?

Transform "if" into "when" by doing first things first. Get up early enough to satisfy your physical and spiritual fitness needs. Do it first—no excuses! Go in later in the morning and spend some time getting the kids off to school, especially if you know you will be home late. Tackle difficult projects first, while you are fresh. Rearrange your schedule consistent with your priorities. Remember, when first things are first, every thing else . . . is second!

Battlefield Lessons on Time Management

Military leaders use the "1/3:2/3 Rule" in allocating sufficient time for subordinates. This battle-tested formula allows no more than 1/3 of the total time available for planning to each headquarters, leaving 2/3 of the time for subordinates to complete their own plans and necessary preparations.

Leaders who are ruthless about the "1/3:2/3 Rule" recognize that "chasing the tail" of perfection—in other words, taking proportionately more time for only incremental returns—robs subordinates of any opportunity to adequately prepare. As we know, there are no "perfect" plans. Time is better spent providing adequate guidance, clear vision, and purpose, while allowing subordinates as much time as possible to be successful.

All of the time management techniques I have learned in the military are designed to create time for leaders to focus on priorities while affording subordinates time to complete their own assignments. I have found that I can operate at what many would consider a breakneck pace, yet do so in a controlled, disciplined tempo, thanks to some of these battle-tested principles:

- "Warning orders" give as much advanced notice as possible of future operations, rather than waiting for a completed plan. Save time by initiating movement toward the objective even before the plan is complete.

- Schedule "open" time on the calendar to get input from others. Time spent face-to-face with subordinate leaders; confirming mission receipt and understanding; measuring progress on milestones and initiatives; assessing climate, values, and personnel issues; and anticipating and fixing small problems before they become large is time well spent.

- Conduct key leader huddles. I like to meet regularly with my closest advisors (chief of staff, operations officer, and sergeant major) to synchronize schedules and allocate time and resources for the top priorities. This is generally done early, before the day begins, or late, in order to synchronize the next day's activities.

- Synchronize watches. Highlight the value of time by emphasizing the importance of precision and discipline. Start and end events on time. Give very specific deadlines for critical actions and hold subordinates accountable.

Leader Business

Leaders must regularly "check alignment"—three-dimensionally. Within the organization, ensure that ends, ways, and means are connected. External to the organization, have good situational awareness and measure alignment with respect to your peers. Assess whether your strategies are mutually supporting, your resources available for sharing. Check alignment with your higher headquarters to ensure that your ends and ways contribute to corporate success.

Conduct frequent listening sessions with your team. If your vision is cloudy, they'll let you know. If they're short on the resources necessary to achieve your goals, you are sure to hear of it. Your willingness to consider others' input should enable the necessary feedback from your three-dimensional team to confirm or deny your alignment.

Leaders must regularly conduct alignment checks with respect to culture and values. If the culture is not consistent with where you are leading your team, change it. Strategic leaders foster a positive culture through training, counseling, personnel actions (hiring and firing), and, as always, leading by example. Communicate regularly with your team about what it will take to achieve your goals and the requisite cultural implications for each team and team member.

Values, however, are generally fixed and non-negotiable. Your ends, ways, and means must be measured against that which you have declared sacrosanct. If your ends are not consistent with your values—change your ends! If the operational procedures necessary to achieve your goals run counter to your values—stop, reassess your ways, or redefine your objectives. If the distribution of means necessary to achieve success runs counter to your beliefs, hold fast to the latter and change the former.

Recognize that time is as important to others (subordinates, customers, teammates, students) as it is to you. Value their time as much as you do your own. Be on time. Get to the point. Make yourself available to answer questions, give guidance, and keep the team moving.

To make the most of your available time, seek balance. Invest in physical and spiritual fitness. Get some rest. Find time for quiet solitude. Take a vacation with your family. Think. Prepare yourself and your team for the long haul.

Strategic leaders know they are in the business of daily organizational alignment. Yes, this includes all that "visionary leadership stuff." Even *The Office*'s Michael Scott gets that part right. But the business of leaders also includes deliberate engagement in the means necessary to achieve that vision, connecting people to the mission, and building a sustainable team that manages resources efficiently and values its members' time. All of this is made possible by the drumbeat of clear, consistent communication and the skillful oversight of the Chief Alignment Officer.

Marching Orders

- *Do you value time—both your own and that of your employees?*

- *What are you doing to solicit input from your teammates to confirm that they have what they need to do their jobs?*

- *If you have too much on your plate, what can you STOP doing?*

- *Is your use of resources sustainable? What sort of investments are you making now with an eye to the future?*

Chapter 9

Living Large in the Empowerment Zone

"Empowerment is all about letting go so that others can get going."
KENNETH BLANCHARD

On a recent Continental Airlines flight, I read with interest in the seat pocket magazine about how the best ideas in this transportation giant "bubbled up" to the top. Top managers seemed genuinely interested in the feedback from workers down in the trenches. People seemed to respond well to the trust they got from their leaders. There was no question from this story about the real sense of commitment to empowerment—and to each other. Tasks were delegated, power was shared, and the team was successful. It was truly inspiring to see the employees respond so well to open, transparent communication and the freedom to operate consistent with the overall company vision and mission.

Many of the Army units I've trained, and no doubt several I've led, don't quite measure up to this standard. Far too often, I have observed junior leaders who failed to make critical decisions because they needed to check with the boss first. For ideas and decisions to be valid, they had to be top-down from the commander. Subordinate leaders were discouraged from providing input to plans and operations. In this environment, people eventually stopped growing and reverted to a "tell me what to do and I'll do it" mentality. These attitudes can be crippling within military units that necessarily rely on subordinate initiative.

No warrior, regardless of his skill in battle, can do it alone. For every General Patton, there was a General Bradley—and a host of other empowered officers—to execute his intentions. Truly effective leaders have to be comfortable operating with subordinates who are empowered to generate good ideas, to take risks, and to determine their own solutions to complex problems. This is the formula for turning *good enough* plans into winning tactics. But it takes leadership to *prepare* people to think and act this way.

The Empowerment Zone

Think of a place where people are inspired, where they have everything they need to accomplish their mission, and where growth and development are available to all. Sounds like Disneyland! Indeed, this is a "happy place" only made possible by the hard preparatory work through which leaders translate plans into action. Even those teams with great employees and all the necessary resources still need the freedom to act and to unleash the greatness within each individual. I call it the *Empowerment Zone*.

Let's face it—this is where we all want to work. It is here in this powerful setting where employees are given the freedom to make decisions, to take action without needing to seek permission, to operate freely with the full backing and consent of their leaders. Employees thrive when they are confident in their abilities and believe that what they are doing adds value. This is the place in which execution through others is possible.

Unfortunately, the Empowerment Zone is all too often an exclusive club. In my experience working with leaders, these conditions describe the organizations that most of us *believe* we have created for our respective teams—but often we have not taken the necessary actions to make it possible. We *hope* we have prepared our teammates to think and operate this way, yet have not made this hope a reality. We *say* they are empowered. Are they really? See if either of these extremes resonates with you:

- Leader A finds himself telling people *how* to do everything. He gets *way* too far down into the weeds (focusing on the tactical problems while neglecting the strategic ones). He will push people out of the way and do things that he had previously delegated. He makes *all* decisions, regardless of the size and scope of the problem. Power is centralized in the hands of one person. This is not empowerment, but dictatorship.

- Leader B is the polar opposite. She delegates everything and then walks away. She offers little in terms of guidance and provides *zero* feedback. She believes she has empowered her team because they have the freedom to decide everything, regardless of their qualifications to do so. She puts people into new positions, hands them an incredibly difficult problem, and pushes them out on a ledge. Then she LEAVES THEM ALONE! Is this empowerment . . . or abandonment?

Remember the expression, "If we don't know where we are going, any road will take us there"? In the Empowerment Zone, leaders are too busy to do other people's job. They have their hands full with the investments in time and energy necessary to pick the right roads and to describe the team's future. Empowering leaders focus on determining the strategic direction of the organization instead of the specific tasks of each team member. They identify *what* must be done and *why*, empowering subordinates to determine *how* to do so.

> "Effective leadership empowers people. The empowerment can be felt in four ways:
> 1. People feel significant.
> 2. Learning and competence matter.
> 3. People are part of a community.
> 4. Work is exciting."
>
> **Warren Bennis**

122

In the Empowerment Zone, leaders get buy-in on plans and strategies from teammates who are included in crafting it. People feel like their leaders listen, that their input matters, and that their unique contribution will enable the success of the team. They receive the necessary skills and tools to make success possible. Work is fun. People will do anything to make victory possible because they are part of something they believe in: a *team*.

I never felt more empowered than during my service as a captain in Germany. My commander gave me enough guidance and coaching to move out, but not so much as to stifle innovation. He made work fun—a difficult task, given the challenges of overseas command! I felt like my input counted, no matter the issue. I felt like I was a part of the plan and therefore would do anything to see it work. I wanted to keep learning in order to contribute to the arena of ideas. I felt comfortable making decisions and, because I interacted with my boss on a regular basis, never perceived his feedback to be a butt-chewing, even when I had missed the mark. While I thought I was on freedom's frontier during the first years of the post-Cold War era, I had no idea I was actually in . . . the Empowerment Zone.

Author Stephen R. Covey describes an empowered organization as one in which teammates have the "knowledge, skill, desire, and opportunity to personally succeed in a way that leads to collective organizational success." In other words, they must have the education to be successful, the opportunities for growth, and the feedback to know they are on the right track.

Education:

People need the necessary skills and tools to operate in the Empowerment Zone. If we want them to make decisions, for example, they need to understand the decision-making process and the intent of their leaders. They need training in order to gain the appropriate level of competence for their position. They need leadership training and communication skills. They need the tools and resources necessary to function. We can't push people out on the ledge without the basic necessities.

In my leadership experience with the military, I generally have had responsibilities commensurate with my training and experience. They did not ask me to command a 15,000-man division as a new lieutenant out of West Point. I wouldn't have known where to start! Instead, I was handed the leadership reins of a 30-man platoon, leaving the Division to officers with 30+ years of experience. Similarly, I did not lead a Corps of Engineers District with a $1B+ budget as a Colonel until I had demonstrated success, at a lower rank, with a much smaller unit.

Since graduating from West Point over 25 years ago, I have been to two combat engineering schools and graduate school at the University of Texas. I have been to Airborne, Air Assault, and Ranger school. I attended the Command and Staff College at Fort Leavenworth and the Army War College. I have been to school for basic staff officers and been given training prior to each level of command. The Army gave me the tools I needed to make decisions, to lead people, and to accomplish the mission. This training has been the basis for empowering me as I moved up to higher levels of responsibility.

Leaders must invest in the development of every member of the team. Formal education programs should be designed based around the skills and tools that are expected of leaders at the next level. In other words, whenever possible, we should not put someone into a position without providing them the necessary enabling skills—first.

Informal education sessions are conducted every day when we talk to our team about how to lead. These discussions include topics such as decision-making, personal and professional growth, business processes, customer satisfaction, new products, or vision. Leaders must spend time with each subordinate and invest in providing the necessary skills and leadership tools that will make them successful.

Opportunity:

Empowerment is realized when we put people in position to grow. Developmental assignments and challenging projects offer people the opportunity to become successful in the empowerment zone. Doing so provides increasingly longer leashes to demonstrate the understanding of how to apply the skills and tools we have afforded them. But let's define the difference between developmental assignments and what we see all too often in traditional, throw-people-to-the-wolves OJT (On the Job Training). The former empowers people to grow and improve. The latter (which is usually much closer to the abandonment model) too frequently leads to failure, disappointment, and disillusionment.

Empowered employees need *increasing* levels of responsibility. These serve as opportunities to evaluate potential and for informal leader development. For the empowered, they stand as future points of reference, with each completed mission providing proof of leadership capacity. Developmental assignments, cross-training, and leadership tasks and roles enable both confidence and competence.

Every day as a cadet at West Point seemed to present another occasion to broaden my leadership tool kit. We sarcastically called them "opportunities to excel." Sometimes it was as simple as standing in class and describing to my classmates how I solved an engineering problem. On other days, I may have had the task of marching a group of 11 cadets to the mess hall for lunch. But every single day served as another chance to test my leadership potential. And the feedback from senior cadets or officers on the staff and faculty, while somewhat painful at the time, helped position me for future success. Every day I, like all 4,000 of my fellow cadets, benefited from multiple opportunities to grow and develop.

Similarly, those 60 hungry days at Ranger School, numerous military deployments and training exercises, and even good old Dr. Lawler's Wastewater Treatment course during my graduate studies at the University of Texas (that one still hurts) all helped prepare me for leadership success. Each one provided some small nugget that would help at some point in my progression. Each represented some degree of investment by my respective leaders in my future growth and development.

To further develop and empower people, we have to do more

than tell them what decisions we have already made. We have to include them in the process of reaching those decisions. As was the case in determining our shared vision, subordinates who feel included in decision-making are significantly more likely to be successful during execution. Those subordinates also become better decision makers of their own, again an investment in growth and development.

We can best give people the chance to be successful in the Empowerment Zone by providing clear problem definitions—and then getting out of the way. In true win/win fashion, the solutions they develop are likely to be better than what might otherwise have been determined without their input. Each opportunity afforded our teammates to solve problems builds confidence and what I like to think of as "leadership muscle mass." We still need to coach, teach, and mentor, but we give people a chance to demonstrate growth and future potential when we step back and let them . . . step up!

Feedback:

Empowering people requires leaders who are willing and able to provide positive, constructive feedback to subordinates. To reach their full potential, our employees and subordinate leaders need to know that they are doing well, meeting (or exceeding expectations), and functioning within our intent. If they are not on the right track, a course correction that provides positive, encouraging alignment makes all the difference.

One way to provide mission-focused feedback is to conduct regular rehearsals. Rehearsals are practice for the whole team, but for the leader especially. They are the key to understanding the concept of operations, confirming subordinate responsibilities, and synchronizing the actions of each team member in time and space. Perhaps most important, they let subordinates know they are on the right track while assuring leaders that their teammates are capable of doing the right thing when placed in various scenarios.

Remember the precision of the attack to liberate Kuwait during Operation Desert Storm? Don't think that fighting and winning a war in 100 hours was the result of chance, good luck, or a weak opponent. It was the byproduct of months of rehearsals at every echelon of every part of the team.

Thousands of us trained in realistic conditions at the Army's training centers and then for months in Kuwait, practicing the very scenarios that we would likely encounter in combat. We rehearsed over maps, in chalk talks and terrain model briefings, and during "live fire" events. While it was clearly not possible to rehearse everything, I had no doubt that we would succeed. The feedback from our leaders at these rehearsals gave us the confidence that we could handle any contingency, and would do so within the framework of the overall battle strategy. We were in the Empowerment Zone.

Leadership author Warren Bennis found that subordinates who undergo significant, meaningful tests emerge "not just stronger, but equipped with the tools he or she needs both to lead and to learn." Leaders cultivate these high-pressure situations, or "crucibles," as growth opportunities, both for themselves and for their teammates.

Most of the great soldiers and leaders demonstrating empowerment and innovation in combat today went through their own "crucibles." For some it may have been the pressure of performing under the watchful eye of a hard drill sergeant in basic training. For others it may have been 60 hungry, tired days at the Army Ranger Course. For many others, it is often the rigors of simulated battle at the National Training Center.

For all of them, the feedback from these training exercises enhances their crucible experience. Units and their leaders gain reference points for use in combat, allowing them to remain calm under pressure. Fundamentally sound, focused on an ever-changing enemy, they are not told what to do, but just to get it done. Under immense pressure every day, these great soldiers and leaders exhibit empowerment with a sort of, "been there, done that" attitude.

The "Just Do It Card"

Subordinates only know they are encouraged to grow, to take risks, and to make decisions when their leaders make it explicitly clear what they are empowered to do—and when they are empowered to do it. I love one empowerment tool in particular: the "Just Do It Card" that General Bob Flowers, former commander of the U.S. Army Corps of Engineers, issued to all 35,000 of his employees. In his organization (and in all of mine since I learned this great technique), all team members were empowered to take appropriate action, without requesting further approval, if they could answer "yes" to the following questions:

1. **Are my actions legal and ethical?** This issue must be addressed first. Employees must understand that they are NOT empowered to take action with a "no." They must also understand that under no circumstances, regardless of the answer to the other questions that follow, will there ever be cause to override this "no." Empowerment must certainly recognize legal and ethical boundaries.

2. **Are my actions good for my customer?** No one knows our customers better than the people who interact with them regularly. Empowered subordinates know that their first-hand understanding of customer needs will enable them to address those requirements without checking higher. Empowered sales associates can adjust prices, make exchanges, etc. Empowered design engineers and architects listen to their customers and adjust plans and specifications accordingly.

3. **Am I willing to be held accountable for my decision?** If it shows up on the front page of the *Washington Post*, or the local paper, can I proudly defend my decision? Am I confident enough in my training and understanding of the problem to put my personal and professional reputation on the line, regardless of the outcome?

4. **Is my action consistent with the team's shared vision?**

THE "JUST DO IT" CARD

Ask these 4 questions:

✓ *Is it legal and ethical?*
✓ *Is it good for my customer?*
✓ *Am I willing to be held accountable for it?*
✓ *Is it consistent with our shared vision?*

If the answer to the 4 questions above is "yes,"
don't ask for permission—you already have it!
Just do it!

The strategic direction, developed corporately with subordinate input, empowers subordinates to determine when and if their individual decisions and actions are a "step" in the same direction.

Remember, all four questions must be answered in the affirmative. A "no" answer to any question is cause for subordinates to take no action or to go higher for permission. But with four "yes" answers, team members must understand that they do not need further permission to take action. They already have it. *Just do i!* Exercising this permission produces individual and organizational growth in empowered risk-takers.

Leader Business

Good communication ensures that the solutions developed by subordinate leaders solve actual problems and help achieve the shared vision. Stay engaged without hovering. Monitor task execution through performance reviews, inspections, and regular dialogue.

Reward success. When subordinates demonstrate empowered decision making, ensure the rest of the team knows it. Show them that you don't simply *allow* such action, you *expect* it.

When empowered teammates come up short, don't punish them without reviewing where *you* might have come up short in preparing them. Have you invested in their training and provided *increasing* levels of responsibility, or are you asking more of them than you should? Are you surprised by subordinate initiatives because you lack consistent communication? Even at their worst, offenses can be used as an opportunity for mutual training and growth.

These are the keys for entering the Empowerment Zone. Providing teammates with education, opportunities, and consistent feedback will indeed serve as the foundation for success in a climate in which people can confidently and capably operate without guidance, make appropriate decisions, and take the sort of aggressive actions that can make good teams great. Force yourself to let go and trust others. I recognize that it can be difficult for passionate leaders, focused on an organization's success, to release some degree of control. But trust me—your subordinates want it. Trust them—they won't let you down.

Marching Orders

* *What keeps you down in the weeds instead of focusing on the bigger picture? Are you afraid to empower others?*

* *Does every member of your team have some sort of career path that includes education and developmental assignments?*

* *Do you give people regular feedback and performance counseling? Is it positive, focusing on how to grow and improve?*

* *Are you confident enough to issue a "Just Do It" Card to your team?*

PART III

EXECUTE

Chapter 10

Leaders Execute

"I think there is something more important than believing: action!
The world is full of dreamers. There aren't enough who will move
ahead and begin to take concrete steps to actualize their vision."
W. CLEMENT STONE

As a major at Fort Hood, Texas I was responsible for the plans and operations of a combat engineer unit. On a training deployment to the NTC with the great Raider Brigade, I had my hat (and my ego) handed to me by the Opposing Force, or OPFOR. For two weeks, the "enemy" found and exploited every weakness in my leadership and warfighting skills, and administered a severe beating to our unit (they really were that good). I am pretty sure that when I completed the training mission, I was at least 20 pounds lighter from a reduction in my backside—courtesy of my boss, Raider 6.

I learned the hard way about the primacy of execution among the responsibilities of the leader. I had briefed Raider 6 on the plan. It was "good enough," with holes that would be filled during execution. The problem was I didn't quite fill all the holes. As an engineer unit, we were responsible for constructing obstacles to disrupt the enemy's attack formations. And we generally did a terrific job of it. One particular operation however, required a very deliberate effort designed to block any possible enemy penetration along our southern flank.

Despite our efforts, they got through. We failed. "Close" was not good enough. I had failed to execute. It's something that still bothers me, truthfully, but of course that is exactly why we trained in the first place. I left the mission with a solid understanding of what it meant to close the deal, to deliver on commitments, and to meet milestones. It reinforced my understanding that no one is ever rewarded for fancy plans, inspiring presentations, or for how they perform in practice. It is all about execution and how we perform when it counts. I got it now—but it still hurts!

Ask your employees what they want from a leader. You'll hear things like vision, compassion, communication, integrity. All good things. We should do all of that. Now ask your supervisor, your shareholders, or your customers the same question. I'll bet you my bottom dollar that they will list traits like performance, results, execution. In business, just like in military operations, it is all about the bottom line. Effective leaders understand that the characteristics on which our teammates place a premium are really only a means to an end. But it is that end—exceeding expectations and successfully completing the mission—that ultimately defines our leadership.

Too many leadership "flavors of the month" lose focus of this fact. Means to getting the job done become ends unto themselves. We can focus on how to be more positive, or how to hold more meaningful meetings, or how to reward employees (again, all good things), but if we can't get the job done or if we don't hit our targets, we miss the point of being in charge.

Author Stephen Covey identified *7 Habits for Highly Effective People*. I have no doubt that were we to follow them, we would be successful: *be proactive; begin with the end in mind; put first things first; think win/win; seek first to understand, then to be understood; synergize; continual improvement*. In fact, I think you will find these same themes are captured here as *Leader Business*. But if we do all of these things, and fail to accomplish the mission, then we are not leading. On the other hand, show me someone who *is* accomplishing the mission, and they are likely following these principles. Thus these elements are *means* to achieving success, not the *ends* that truly count. No matter what, we must keep the end in mind: mission accomplishment.

Leadership is about making things happen, incorporating best practices, and constantly improving each individual as well as the team. *Planning* and *preparation* (and all the duties that support those stages)—in other words, everything we have talked about so far—must result in a better, cheaper, faster, safer product or service. We can't get so wrapped up in *how* to lead that we miss out on *why* we lead! The business of leaders is to win, to get the job done, and to accomplish the mission. There should be no doubt about this #1 leadership responsibility.

Back in Ranger School, we often rotated leadership positions within my patrol after *planning* and *preparations* for the mission were complete. One Ranger would be graded based on how those phases of the mission went, and then another would be in the hot seat for evaluation during execution.

There was no finger-pointing and no blaming my predecessor. As the new patrol leader during the execution phase, if I didn't like the plan, it was up to me to change it. My mission was clear: get to the objective and destroy the enemy, take care of my people, finish the job, and be ready to fight again. The details of how we had planned to be successful, or whether we had effectively prepared, were minor considerations once we entered into the arena. Our focus was the mission—and only the mission. My job was to get it done. No questions, no whining, no excuses.

"There are two kinds of people: those who do the work and those who take the credit. Try to be in the first group; there is less competition there."

Indira Gandhi

Military operations are, by their nature, chaotic. We always pick the worst terrain and weather conditions. The enemy never seems to cooperate. Subordinates lose focus (in Ranger School they were either thinking about food or sleep . . . or both!). Our job as leaders is to bring order out of that chaos. We establish intermediate objectives, milestones, metrics, and measurements to monitor progress and ensure we are on a glidepath for victory. We make constant adjustments to our operation based on the situation; we are totally focused on the mission, yet flexible in how we accomplish it. We peer through the ever-present "fog of war" and keep our respective units headed in the right direction.

As district commander (CEO) for the Army Corps of Engineers, I was in execution mode from day one on the job and from minute one each day. We were accountable to customers and stakeholders for projects worth hundreds of millions of dollars. Our diverse business lines varied from environmental protection to military construction. Hundreds of projects in different phases of completion were continually competing for limited resources. Once again, it was organized chaos—in that sense, no different from a combat unit or a leadership role in any other field. My job was to sort through the friction in order to accomplish the mission.

Leaders Execute

Part III of *Leader Business* is "Leaders Execute." In this section we will examine the difference-making skills and attributes that focus first and foremost on mission accomplishment. *Planning* and *preparation* merely set the conditions for success. Tangible proof of leadership excellence is only gained by men and women in the arena who come out victorious. *Execution* is the sum of those leadership tasks that focus on the primary leader responsibility of getting the job done.

It begins with an examination of no-excuse leadership. I call this "less '*hooah*,' more '*dooah*.'" Leaders understand that they are graded on performance, not on good intentions. All the inspirational speeches, fancy presentations, and slick marketing pieces become irrelevant once it is time to get the job done. Execution then, is the time to move past the bravado and make stuff happen.

Many leaders, military and civilian, forget this. We say that they "brief well"—code for someone who can speak eloquently but can't deliver on it. They puff their chests up and talk a good game, then disappear when it is time to go to work. These are the leaders among us who emphasize process over product, delivery over deliverables, and morale over mission. They miss the point of effective leadership: get the job done.

Don't get me wrong. All the other stuff—process, presentation, planning, and preparation—is important. We cannot just jump in without the leadership tasks that enable success. But it is meaningless if leaders cannot execute. Effective leaders therefore, focus less on themselves and their individual success (i.e. less "*hooah*," the sort of cheer that military warriors use to get people excited about the mission) and more on the overall success of the team (more "*dooah*"). In other words, they care less about *looking* good than actually *being* good.

Let me break it down this way. I like to think that there is a way to demonstrate laser-like focus on the mission that helps people understand what it means to execute. This approach applies to any mission, any task, or any assignment. These are the three rules for business or military mission success:

1. **Focus on the enemy.** In other words, it is always about the mission—not process or format. We need to move all other concerns to the back burner and stay aligned with whatever it takes to be successful.

2. **Fight the enemy, not the plan.** Stuff happens. How we deal with it defines our leadership. Our plans are a point of departure, a means to the end, *not* the end itself.

3. **When in doubt, see Rule #1.** Got it?

OK, perhaps this is a little extreme. But for a warfighter, this sort of focus is necessary to ensure people keep their heads up, respond to changing conditions, and keep things in context. Poor tactical leaders are infamous for excusing their actions by saying something like,

"Well . . . the plan *said* I was supposed to do that, so I did it." Really? Even if it no longer made any sense? Even if it contributed nothing to our overall goals? Even if it meant that 100% completion of your assigned tasks contributed *zero* to the mission? This business of leaders is a thinking man/woman's game. Execution is what we think about! Remember: less "hooah," more "dooah!"

So let's examine the leadership skills and attributes that enable successful execution. Leaders communicate

> *"Vision without action is a daydream. Action without vision is a nightmare."*
>
> **Japanese Proverb**

effectively—focused on the mission. They are decisive, no matter the situation. This is especially true in times of crisis, when leadership truly matters. Successful leaders have great situational awareness (we will discuss SA shortly) and position themselves at the critical time and place to influence the action. They execute through empowered subordinates, with "spider senses" that anticipate problems and avoid crises.

As a trainer at the NTC, the best leaders with whom I worked had a laser-like focus when it came to execution. My job was to follow them around the battlefield, monitor their conversations with subordinates, and understand their decision-making. With the good ones it was almost impossible to keep up. They were constantly communicating—by FM radio, text message, or face-to-face. They were always on the move and, not coincidentally, always at the spot on the battlefield where they could most powerfully influence the action. They invested in planning and preparation, but they knew that they would be successful only if they had a measurable impact on the accomplishment of the mission.

In the military and in business, these leadership responsibilities are all connected during execution. Leaders who circulate the battlefield are constantly communicating and have the situational awareness they need to make decisions during execution. They are always "up on the net," talking to subordinates about what they see and enabling the situational awareness of the entire team. Cross-talk and communication among an empowered team of teams helps anticipate problems and minimize the impact of pending crises.

Leader Business

Leaders who focus on execution have an unquenchable commitment to excellence. They are not satisfied with second place, with *almost*, or with *pretty good* (except in their plans, of course!). They want to win. They want their team to succeed. They want to be the best in every measurable category. To accept anything less than perfection is viewed as an invitation for failure. That's not something to be entertained . . . ever!

At the NTC, I led units through a deliberate examination of their performance called an "After Action Review" (we'll cover AARs in depth in Part IV). We focused almost exclusively on execution in these post-mission debriefs. Yes, we could have talked forever about the holes in the plan and about which member of the staff should be summarily hanged . . . but that discussion, while temporarily satisfying (for everyone except that poor staff member), wasn't sufficient to get to the heart of a unit's problems. I kept the focus on who did what with regard to completing the mission. Our AARs focused principally on the fundamental elements of execution: communication, leader positioning, decision-making, and establishing conditions for subordinate success. The goal was nothing less than perfection. We talked much more about what went wrong—what kept us from perfection—than what we did well. In the end, we wanted to win every battle, 100-0.

Poor leaders often chafed under the rigors of self-criticism and the detailed examination of shortcomings. Great leaders, however, loved the opportunity to expose every weak node in the system and to determine how to correct them. Poor leaders wanted to know how many of the enemy they killed. Great ones wanted to know how many got away and what they could have done to destroy every last one of them. Poor leaders tried to understand why their subordinates failed. Great ones wanted to understand what they could have done to help their teammates execute successfully.

One of the best books on execution is titled, appropriately enough, *Execution: The Discipline of Getting Things Done.* Here's how authors Larry Bossidy and Ram Charan describe the relation between execution and the other themes of *Leader Business*:

> "Everybody talks about change. In recent years, a small industry of changemeisters has preached revolution, reinvention, quantum change, breakthrough thinking, audacious goals, learning organizations, and the like. We're not necessarily debunking this stuff. But unless you translate big thoughts into concrete steps for action, they're pointless. Without execution, the breakthrough thinking breaks down, learning adds no value, people don't meet their stretch goals, and the revolution stops dead in its tracks. What you get is change for the worse, because failure drains the energy from your organization. Repeated failure destroys it."

Vision, planning, preparations, learning—all are for naught if the mission is not accomplished. Nothing else really matters. Companies become irrelevant overnight. They die with good mission statements, but no mission. Leaders are responsible for keeping their team's collective eye on the ball, to focus on being successful, however that is measured.

Successful leaders, in business and in the military, do this by linking everything to the mission. *Planning* is necessary to align people and processes, with the necessary resources, to accomplish the mission. *Preparation* is completed to confirm readiness to accomplish the mission. Leaders infuse a passion for *learning* throughout the team to make them better prepared for future mission success.

Execution requires leaders to follow up and follow through. An action passed along to someone else is not an action *completed.* Systems must be established (metrics, milestone reviews, inspections, evaluations) to monitor progress. Empowered subordinate leaders must understand the importance of proactive, open communication to highlight progress toward objectives, while at the same time identifying needs for assistance and possible emerging opportunities.

Let me be honest here. This sort of total focus is what makes leadership so exhausting . . . and exhilarating. It takes every ounce of our energy . . . and makes it fun. After all, we all want to win; we all want to see people succeed and reach their personal and professional goals.

Of course that kind of laser focus isn't easy. Even with all my experience, I still miss the mark every once in a while. I take my eye off the ball. I put energy into ways and means and forget about the ends. This was definitely the case during that fateful mission at the NTC, when I failed to meet Raider 6's very clear guidance on how he wanted to fight the enemy. I put a ton of energy into the plan. I ensured that the resources were where they needed to be. I issued orders and instructions to subordinate leaders.

But *I* didn't follow up. And when I learned—too late—that we had not completed our assignments, and we were in full crisis mode, I was too slow in generating options. Before I could recover, the enemy penetrated our position and was driving circles around our rear area units. Not a good day.

I don't think I'll ever forget the lessons of that training battle. It is truly all about execution. The men and women I have led in combat operations could care less about how good we looked on paper. The customers I have served in a billion dollar organization felt the same about our strategic plan or our efforts to improve employee morale. In each case, all they wanted was to succeed, to win, to get what they expected in terms of products and services. This will always be the case, no matter the environment in which we do battle. Somehow everything else loses importance when the enemy is penetrating our position, when market share is lost, when share price declines, and when business units fail. Execution is the primary responsibility of the leader. Period.

Marching Orders

- *Does your organization have an unquenchable desire for excellence?*

- *How do you monitor execution?*

- *What is the nature of your personal and organizational communication? Does it focus on execution?*

- *Do you have the situational awareness necessary to anticipate problems, position key leaders, and make decisions?*

- *Are you a crisis warrior? Do you have the skills and tools necessary to execute under pressure?*

Chapter 11

Less "Hooah," More "Dooah!"

"It is time for us all to stand and cheer for the doer, the achiever—
the one who recognizes the challenge and does something about it."
VINCE LOMBARDI

If you're like me—Type A, competitive, driven, goal-oriented—
there's a better-than-average chance that you turned to this chapter first! (If you did, go back to the beginning. The other stuff
does matter!) But this truly is what being in charge is all about: accomplishing the mission. Everything else is an enabler. It is *how* we
get to the objective, how we *set the conditions* to be successful. We
can have great plans, big vision, or amazing people with sky-high
morale. All of these are good things, but ultimately it comes down to
whether or not we get the job done.

I enjoy speaking to leaders, especially first-level supervisors
and people in their first management position. I try to get them to
give me their nominations for the number one priority of a leader. I
will intentionally focus in on those common themes surrounding taking care of people. "That's number one, right: taking care of our employees? I can't think of anything more important, don't you agree?"
Then, once I've got all the heads nodding north and south, I bring the
hammer: *"Wrong! The first priority is to accomplish the mission!"*

Mind you, this is a leading question. We know that taking care
of people and accomplishing the mission are so interrelated that it is
really not possible to do one without the other. It's just like the need
to plan and prepare before we can enter into the arena. I get that.
But make no mistake—the business of leaders is to accomplish the

mission, no matter what it takes! It is about making decisions, solving problems, adjusting people, processes, and resources while "in the fight," and dealing with crisis situations. This is undoubtedly the largest component of our performance objectives and the basis for measuring our leadership abilities. It is all about *execution*!

BE – KNOW – DO

I have been fortunate to receive formal leadership education in settings like West Point; Basic and Advanced Engineering at Fort Belvoir, Virginia; Command and Staff College at Fort Leavenworth, Kansas; and Army Ranger training at Fort Benning, Georgia. Each of these schools emphasized different aspects of technical and tactical competence and, more importantly, leadership. Ranger School and West Point emphasized leadership of small, elite units. Command and Staff College provided perspectives on leading larger, more complex, multi-service operations. Each was important in shaping my perspectives on what we expect from our leaders.

Field Manual 22-100, the U.S. Army's basic leadership doctrine, has been a common thread throughout. It defines the roles and responsibilities of an Army leader and has given me a fantastic framework for the critical components of military leadership. Its BE-KNOW-DO philosophy has helped shape a generation of Army leaders like me. It is the basis for character-based, competent leadership—and a model that works beyond the military:

- **BE** (Provide character-based leadership to the organization.)

- **KNOW** (Know your job and be competent in your profession.)

- **DO** (Accomplish the mission and take care of your people.)

Note that the first two elements in this leadership framework are passive (or internal) qualities; the third, meanwhile, is action-oriented. It is through this component, the "doing," that great leaders are recognized. We can *be* a good person, but if we fail to accomplish the mission, we are not leading. We can *know* an encyclopedic amount of information but fail as a leader because we cannot get the job done. Certainly we want all three. But, first and foremost, we had better be "doers!"

> *"A leader is one who knows the way, goes the way and shows the way."*
>
> **John C. Maxwell**

As I've mentioned, I'm a competitive person. No matter the setting, I want my team to win. I want us to exceed our goals. I want to see my teammates recognized for being great. I want to keep raising the bar, setting increasingly higher goals and objectives, and keep pushing my team to new performance records. I want to do my job, be a good leader, help my teammates by enabling their success, and be part of an organization that is never content with second place.

I don't think I fully embraced this until I led an engineer company in Germany. Perhaps my new attitude had something to do with the little detour to Fort Benning I took prior to my new assignment—and the new Ranger tab I wore on my left shoulder. My own "crucible" experience may have generated a newfound confidence in my abilities and recognition of what an empowered, competent team could do. Or it might have simply been the maturity of my new rank (captain) and the recognition that people were counting on me with their lives.

Whatever it was, the lights came on for me when I was given the responsibility of a hundred men and their families, and a mission that could not fail. I wanted my team to be the best: highest physical fitness test scores, best on the rifle range, highest reenlistment rate, and recognition as the most tactically sound sapper company in the battalion. I believed in myself and in my troopers and translated this *confidence* into a shared sense of *competence* that reflected my desire not only to compete, but to win. We did. No one messed with the

Alpha Company "Outlaws!"

This same formula translated into success when it was time for me to lead civilians in Detroit and Los Angeles. I wanted to be recognized as the best Army Corps of Engineers District in the nation. I wanted my team to replace "we think we can" with "we know we will," to never accept anything less than 100% mission accomplishment. I wanted a culture in which we would embrace the hairiest of challenges, never quit until we were successful, and never make excuses for poor performance. As I write these words, I think we are there!

No matter the setting or the operational context, people excel when they are confident in their leaders. Our challenge is to gain this confidence and become a take charge, action-oriented, make-things-happen kind of leader. We want to look good on paper because we *are* good on the ground. We want to be where the action is (start at the B.F.T. and expand from there). We want to proficiently solve problems and adjust resources. It is a pretty simple motto: "Less hooah, more dooah!" Leadership, my friends, is an action verb.

Lead From the Front

Leaders set the example in their words and, more importantly, in their actions. Those who execute best are out in front, teaching and mentoring, and modeling character and the values of the organization in all that they do. We can't do this from behind closed doors. Nor can we do this by hiding behind emails and office memorandums. We have to get out of the office and down on the shop floor. We have to spend time with our teammates, understand their issues, and enable their success. We have to identify and get to the greatest points of friction and be ready with a heavy dose of grease. That is leading from the front.

Among history's great "lead-from-the-front" military leaders, perhaps none stands as tall as German Field Marshal Erwin Rommel. His tactics were considered unconventional by his contemporaries. Rather than issue commands from the comfort of a headquarters in the rear area, Rommel chose to be with his troops, as close as possible to the action. He was famous for rolling up his sleeves and lending a hand to his men, no matter the task.

Perhaps some day, history will view David Petraeus as this generation's archetypal lead-from-the-front general. While most deployments to Iraq and Afghanistan are for 12 months, General Petraeus has spent the better part of a decade in the Middle East. Commanding units ranging from the "Screaming Eagles" of the 101st Airborne Division to all forces in the Iraq and Afghanistan theater of operations, General Petraeus continues to validate the premise that you cannot lead effectively from the rear.

Another less well-known individual who excels at leading from the front and practicing "dooah" leadership is Michael Chasen. As CEO of the education software provider Blackboard, when one of his operating divisions was going through a difficult period, he packed up his desk and moved in with the low performing team. Chasen knew where the action was, and knew the value of his presence. Once the unit was back on its feet, he stepped back, always ready to go where the action was—just like Rommel, just like Petraeus.

The Army definition of leadership is "*influencing* people by *providing* purpose, direction, and motivation while *operating* to *accomplish* the mission and *improving* the organization." Note the action verbs in the definition. You cannot lead men and women in business from behind a desk or by email any more than you can command troops in battle without constant, consistent, energetic, mission-focused, lead-from-the-front activity.

This is "dooah" leadership. Leaders are in the arena, where victories are gained and champions are made. They accomplish the mission and improve the teams they lead, focusing not just on achieving short-term improvements, but rather lasting excellence. They are decisive, especially in times of crisis. With every task, they seek to be their absolute best, never accepting less than 100%, and will do anything necessary, provided it is both moral and ethical, to get there. This is the number one priority of a leader. Everything else, while important, is not number one. Any questions so far?

It's the Mission, Stupid

The philosophy of that cultural icon Larry the Cable Guy says it all: *Git 'er done!* Leaders get the job done. All the hype, positive spin, and self-promotion in the world cannot compensate for a lack of results.

Leaders develop milestones and metrics that contribute to mission accomplishment. They establish regular review mechanisms to ensure that the team is on track. They hold themselves and their team accountable for mission accomplishment, assessing goals and objectives during each performance review. It's a simple framework for these frequent discussions: Did we accomplish the mission: yes or no? If yes, then move to how to raise the bar. If no, hold people accountable (including yourself) and listen for ways to improve performance.

On the other hand, it is simply not enough to accomplish the mission and achieve short-term goals and objectives. "Git 'er done" leaders cannot be so myopic that they neglect the long term viability of the teams they lead. Unfortunately, many are the leaders who have run their organizations into irrelevancy in pursuit of quarterly earnings, immediate results, and instant gratification.

> *"I am a verb, not a noun."*
>
> **Ulysses S. Grant**

There is a better, more balanced, approach. Great leaders recognize that they must have a long-term vision that develops the entire organization in order to sustain greatness. Immediate actions and initiatives must be aligned with the more distant goals and objectives. True leadership is about "gittin 'er done" over the long haul.

When I think of this sort of balance, I think of how I was trained to operate as a vehicle commander in a Humvee, leading a small crew from the right front seat. I was taught that we have to constantly adjust the focus of our eyes, to be ever vigilant in scanning for approaching hazards, changing environmental conditions, indicators of potential attack. We have to refocus to see problems closer at hand: potholes, roadside bombs, or insurgent activity. It is definitely a balance. Focus on the front tires and we'll miss the opportunity to avoid the trouble ahead. Lean too far forward and we'll miss the land mine that the front tires just ran over!

I have tried to lead my various teams with this same sort of balance. Discussions of metrics, overhead accounts, or daily/weekly/monthly revenues can only be a piece of our oversight. We must similarly look over the horizon and ensure we are meeting our strategic, long-range goals. Initiatives that develop skills for the future or foster new relationships for emerging business opportunities have to be an equal part of our drive to execute. We have to measure them and held each other accountable, just as we do for our short-range requirements.

As leaders, we are charged with improving everything entrusted to us. This is perhaps the greatest shortcoming in the all-too-common "results now" approach to leadership. The mission may be accomplished, but at what cost? Our own personal success may be assured, but at what price for the organizations we lead?

Leaders must understand that mission success has to be sustainable. People, processes, and systems must be established to ensure that quarterly success is repeatable—quarter after quarter, year after year. To do so, we must execute the mission in ways that make our people, facilities, equipment, and the very communities that we serve better than when we entered into our respective positions. We have to balance our time, energy, and resources in each of these areas to ensure a sustainable competitiveness:

- **People.** Leaders improve people through training, mentorship, and challenging assignments. We must pursue every opportunity to improve the skills of our teammates, through both traditional and non-traditional developmental programs.

- **Facilities.** When we examine our workspaces, do they contribute to teamwork? Do our facilities positively shape collaborative behavior? Are they better than when we inherited them, and do they support the business we envision in the next one, five, or 10 years?

- **Equipment.** Do our subordinates have the necessary tools to remain competitive? What investments must we at least initiate to enable the type of work our organization must execute in the future? Can't afford it all right now? Who can? Let's get started.

- **Community.** Consider that our organizations are part of a bigger team that includes our customer base and the very communities that we serve. How can we have a measurable impact and demonstrate a vision for something even bigger than just our company or team? Investments in this area are not simply for humanitarian purposes or for tax write-offs. They often return benefits many times greater than their cost.

Shifts Happen!

As Field Marshal Rommel famously said, "No plan survives first contact with the enemy." This is fundamental to being able to accomplish the mission. While our plans are important, we need to be prepared to make adjustments once our plans meet reality. We have to understand our environment, know the positioning and capabilities of our team, see opportunities and threats as they present themselves, and be ready for action. Shifts happen!

Leaders add value by demonstrating confidence in their ability to make decisions and adjust plans when required. There will always be friction. How we respond to it, how we leverage it to an advantage, and how we execute the mission—no matter what—is perhaps the single most important defining measurement of our leadership competence.

In the chaos following Hurricane Katrina in 2005, no one better exemplified decisive leadership than the U.S. Army's Lieutenant

General Russel L. Honore. Remembered for his straight shooting on CNN ("That's B.S." he responded to one interview question. "You're stuck on stupid!") and his ever-present cigar, General Honore was a clear example of decisive, take-charge leadership. This guy walked around with a 10-gallon can of grease, ready to deal with any friction that came his way!

How did someone like General Honore succeed where others failed? He was battle-tested, mission-focused, and decisive. He assessed the situation, identified what needed to be done, established priorities, and made things happen. I've seen the guy in action when I trained some of his units out at the NTC. It was clear to me that his ability to get control of the situation in New Orleans, to deal with "shifts," was simply an extension of what he learned dealing with chaos in the military.

What can we learn from General Honore and his "take charge" approach in New Orleans? Here are a few lessons from the "Ragin' Cajun" that can be applied to any situation in which unexpected issues arise:

1. Understand your environment.

I've seen the General at work on the battlefield and watched knowingly as he moved throughout the flood-damaged areas of New Orleans. No one I've ever served with has a better sense for "being where the action is." The point is, there is no substitute for first hand information. We have to get into the trenches and find out what is happening. We gain insights by listening to our subordinate leaders, sales staff, factory floor workers, and all those who will be affected by our decisions (our customers in the broadest sense). We deal with chaos first by understanding the source of the problem and the capabilities of our team to deal with it.

2. Realign the team.

One of my favorite descriptions of a key responsibility of leaders is, in true General Honore-speak, to "un-confuse the situation." Success in execution is gained through leaders who can identify what is decisive and sort out priorities. Assess your people and their current status. Identify your resource requirements and see if they are aligned against your top priorities. Make adjustments based on an understanding of strengths, weaknesses, opportunities and threats. Communicate changes and keep moving toward the objective.

3. Take charge!

Few will forget the sight of the General strolling the streets of New Orleans, barking orders to soldiers, first responders, and almost anyone else within earshot. General Honore followed the time-tested lesson: When in charge, take charge! Make adjustments to the plan, communicate them to those who will execute them, and stay focused on the mission.

Execution Warriors

Successful mission accomplishment is usually the result not of one big decision that carries the day, but rather a series of smaller ones that add up to victory. Still, most of those decisions need to yield positive results. *Execution* warriors are leaders who thrive in the arena, who enjoy the game as much as the victory, and who demonstrate in their "dooah!" that they are up to the task. These are the leaders whom people follow: confident, competent, and capable decision makers.

> *"Even if you are on the right track, you will get run over if you just sit there."*
>
> ***Will Rogers***

How does a leader gain experience in decision-making? By making decisions, of course! Why was a general schooled in the principles of battle tactics successful on the flood-ravaged "battlefields" of the bayou? Years and years of practice. If you are looking for a magical transition to superhero leader status, you won't find it here. Successful execution comes from multiple repetitions of decision-making. Think of it as increasing your leadership muscle density.

Here are some exercises that will build your leadership muscles:

1. ***Conduct a war-game.*** Part of any rigorous decision-making process, a war-game is an exercise designed to visualize an operation in time and space to help predict its outcome. At its best, conducted on a map or using a computer simulation tool, a war-game synchronizes "friendly" actions and anticipates responses against potential operational challenges (the "enemy," terrain and weather issues, media, resource constraints, etc.) Leader participation in war-games as part of the planning process allows for the opportunity to visualize the future battlefield and, most importantly, to pre-identify any potential decision points. Let's count this as repetition number one.

2. ***Conduct rehearsals.*** Consider these the practice sessions before the big game. Best when executed in conditions that closely replicate the future battlefield, rehearsals give leaders the opportunity to practice making the decisions associated with the pre-identified decision points. This is repetition number two.

3. ***Execute.*** Make decisions. Take charge. Know that as the leader you are expected to make decisions—so make them! Know that some decisions will be good and some will be, well, not so good. But also know that leader growth only comes from the willingness to place yourself in the arena and execute.

4. ***Review your decisions.*** Be willing to participate in a "no thin skins" examination of what you did, why you did it, and how you can improve. As a leader, focus on the information that shaped your decisions and who provided it to you, how you communicated your decision to subordinates, and what you did to reinforce your decision to ensure successful ex-

ecution. (We'll talk more about these sorts of reviews in Part IV.) This is repetition number four. Now feel your leadership muscles. Not bad, eh? This is how execution warriors like Gen. Honore get so strong!

Leader Business

Be bold and decisive in your execution, but do so consistent with a shared vision. This is the road map within which each shift and every decision must make sense. If it doesn't, you are confusing the situation—not "un-confusing" it. Take every opportunity to frame your decisions within the larger context of where you are taking the team. Check your alignment and ensure that people and resources are consistent with organizational priorities, immediate actions contribute to strategic goals and objectives, and that tasks contribute to the overall mission. Make shifts only when they are a step toward the goal line.

Leaders know that there are often impediments to positive communication. The urgency of the situation often requires that subordinates subject themselves to our influence without the sharing of all elements of purpose, direction, and motivation. Sometimes they just need to do what we tell them to do. They will if they trust us.

Do not believe that simply because of our position, subordinates will trust our judgment and decision-making. We must earn their confidence. This is enabled by open communication, participative decision-making, and results. When we demonstrate that we are trustworthy ("dooah!"), we will be trusted.

Most importantly, stay calm under pressure. Treat issues like they are a matter of life and death only if they are. Leaders who are able to execute even in the most chaotic situations, and who remain under control no matter the situation, convey confidence to the rest of the team. Creating an environment of trust among teammates assures subordinates of our willingness to empower them to deal with the situation, to understand the issues more fully before reaching conclusions, and to keep any crisis in the appropriate perspective.

If execution was easy, remember, we wouldn't need leaders.

But there will always be crises. No leader and no organization in pursuit of the big prizes can consistently operate without some setbacks. So get comfortable being uncomfortable. Make decisions, adjust your plan, stay focused, and accomplish the mission. Find a way and "git 'er done!"

Marching Orders

- *Does your team have an unquenchable desire for excellence? If not, how can you lead by example and make them believe?*

- *How do you monitor execution? Do you have clear metrics, and are they tied to individual performance goals and objectives?*

- *Are you getting the necessary information to anticipate problems, position key leaders, and make decisions?*

- *Are you getting enough decision-making repetitions to be effective at this critical leadership task?*

Chapter 12
Warrior Communication

"In combat, if you can't communicate, you're just camping out."
GENERAL **J.D. THURMAN**

At the completion of every training event at the National Training Center (NTC), the standard procedure was for my trainers to report to me with their top leadership issues. I wanted to know what sort of feedback I could share with my counterpart, the training unit commander. I was looking for themes common among his subordinate leaders and areas that might help him understand how to improve his unit's execution. Almost without exception, my team would highlight communication as their top issue.

Just like business executives, military leaders are consistently challenged with an inability to make decisions and execute successfully because they lack clarity on issues. Generally this is because people are not sharing information or, when they do, it is incomplete or not timely. Commanders usually find it difficult to command when they cannot "see" the battlefield and lack the common picture that is the result of consistent, transparent communication. This is how, as General Thurman so eloquently put it, warriors are reduced to campers. There really isn't much else to do when people aren't talking to each other.

These themes are consistent in every command in which I have served and in every leadership group I have spoken to about the business of leaders. Communication issues were the dominant issue in my subordinate trainers' reports and are what continue to befuddle combat (and business) leaders in every setting. Radio channels (or whatever means of sharing data) are silent and life is seemingly good—until subordinates are in full crisis mode; cross-talk among subordinate leaders is infrequent, with none of the sharing of successes and failures that can aid organizational improvement and mission accomplishment; teams routinely lack clarity about goals and objectives, and tackle their tasks without a clear understanding of the team's shared vision; and people long for the sort of positive feedback that inspires greatness and keeps tasks aligned with the overall strategic purpose.

Stop me if you've heard this before . . . because I'm guessing we're describing your organization (and mine). Communication is all too frequently the most pressing execution issue preventing us from being our best.

What is so darned hard about communication? Such a seemingly simple skill, practiced by most of us since early childhood, serves as a consistent source of frustration for leaders everywhere. It sure does seem to be a universal leadership challenge. We see communication issues in every facet of our leadership journey:

- Plans and instructions are not shared with teammates.

- Counseling and performance feedback does little to develop subordinates.

- Leaders don't know what their team is doing to enable mission accomplishment—and vice versa.

- People continue to repeat errors and make the same mistakes, evidence of a failure to share lessons learned and cultivate a learning environment.

Nothing impacts execution like a failure to communicate. Yet, as most of us will agree, there is no more valued element within a team. People want to be informed. They want feedback, to know if they are on the right track, and to know that their efforts are valued. Leaders want to understand early when there are problems so they can make timely decisions.

Let there be no doubt: communication before, during, and after each mission is the key to successful execution and mission accomplishment. You can overcome bad plans with good communication. You can account for poor preparations with good communication. But if your *comms* are bad, you're not leading the attack—you really are just camping out.

Communication Breakdown

In my experience, communication shortcomings are either *hardware* or *software* issues. The former can involve telecommunication infrastructure (phones, wireless tools, radios, networks, etc.) and the means with which these tools operate and talk to each other. While sometimes a bit expensive, they are usually the easiest to fix.

It is the software issues that are the more difficult ones to tackle. Our IT support people don't have the solutions here. These software issues are a reflection of how each of us are wired, how we process information, and the communication that enables mission accomplishment. These are the softer leadership issues of personal interaction, of clear communication, of understanding and being understood. Together, communication hardware and software help enable our respective team's success.

Let's start with the easy part. In this technologically advanced age, there *are* usually solutions to our communication hardware issues. Proven leaders often go through this simple set of questions, the answers to which will provide the framework for our communication requirements:

1. What decisions do we need to be able to make?

2. What are our information requirements in order to make them?

3. How will we gain access to this information and share it with each other?

4. What hardware will our team need in order to enable our decision making and create a common view of the situation?

Sure seems easy, doesn't it? Not so fast! Does this information need to be sent through secure means? Does it need to be stored so that others can use it? Is either the sender or receiver(s) in areas where various means of communications might be challenged—say, for example, in mountains, heavy forest, or the Upper Peninsula of Michigan? Can the required information be sent by voice or data lines? Can it be sent digitally or by overnight express mail?

Effective leaders must get involved early in these kinds of hardware issues. Too many times at the NTC and in the private sector, battles are won or lost because, when the critical time comes for the leader to make a decision, she is limited by her communications hardware. Resources are left on the table, available but unallocated. Personnel are misaligned against changing conditions.

We saw this issue at its worst during and right after the blast to the Gulf Coast that was Hurricane Katrina. The absence of landlines, cellular telephone towers, and satellite phones (and no backup plan) created an almost complete lack of situational awareness—both on the ground and in command centers from New Orleans to Washington, DC. First responders could not communicate with other support agencies. Responsibilities could not be assigned. Resources, supplies, and troops could not be apportioned to meet requirements. The result was chaos.

In military operations, one technique I have used to demonstrate the importance of hardware issues is to have my team show me how we will have communication across the full width and depth of the battlefield—*before* they brief me on the proposed battle plan. Where are the critical communication relay nodes? Where will we have voice, data, and satellite coverage—and where will we have to assume risk? These issues are as important to me as the actual battle plan. In my experience, it makes little difference how impressive the tactics might be if our hardware fails to get us to the fight.

Most of our endeavors are no different. Data systems don't talk to each other. Servers get overloaded, email systems crash, and people cannot access the network from remote locations. No matter the setting, these are major problems and roadblocks to successful execution. But we can learn two things from this discussion. One is that these hardware issues *are* solvable. Expensive . . . but they are solvable. The second is this: Most of our communication challenges are not technology related. It's much softer.

Author Jim Collins cautions that technology will not be the final solution: "*When used right, technology becomes an accelerator of momentum, not a creator of it.*" In other words, we have to know what we are doing—first. We must have solid processes and procedures before technology can make a difference. Technology is a *means* to an end, not an *end* in and of itself.

> "The key to success is to get out into the store and listen to what the associates have to say. It's terribly important for everyone to get involved. Our best ideas come from clerks and stock boys."
>
> **Sam Walton**

Which technologies are important for communication? Those that *facilitate* the softer issues of leaders making decisions. It's almost paradoxical but the softer issues are usually the hardest ones to address. But take heart—many of these solutions cost next to nothing to implement.

Sometimes it is as straightforward as this: People simply need to understand how important it is that they communicate. But they only know this when we tell them. So let's begin by telling them! Subordinates have a tendency to assume (often wrongly) that we have our own way of obtaining information. They often assume (again, wrongly) that their leaders do not want to be bothered with pieces of information but want to be informed once the problem is solved (or not). We need to ensure that they know what we want to know, when we want to know it, and how we want this information shared with us.

I have seen this far too often in combat. Subordinates wait to try to figure everything out on their own, coming up on the net when it is too late for anyone to help. When radio nets are silent, leaders typically assume that all is well, only to learn later that those early indicators of trouble were never elevated. Too often information is held at lower levels because subordinates are afraid to communicate potentially bad news or are unaware of our desire to be part of the problem solving process. They only know this . . . when we tell them.

I have found that sometimes even "nothing significant to report" is tactically significant: *"Bushmaster 6, this is Dog 6. I am at Check Point 2. No change to our mission. No significant enemy activity. Our resources are green (good). We are continuing the mission."*

People have to understand that even this sort of "nothing to report" transmission is important. With this kind of routine communication, it is much easier to visualize what is happening across the team, determine where we need to be to influence critical events, anticipate decisions, and position our resources. On their own, subordinates probably won't communicate. It is our job to help them understand how important it is that we all stay up on the net. Information is power. Communication is the key.

Walk into many command posts in the Army and you will see the following sign posted over the map, near the radio, and over the computers: *"Who else needs to know?"* It is a reminder that someone may gain an advantage from knowing what we know. Often it is the seemingly trivial piece of information, discounted by the recipient, which can determine the outcome of an operation.

Someone, somewhere—higher, lower, left flank, right flank—needs to know what we know. Perhaps it is the unit commander, an adjacent organization, or our higher headquarters that would benefit from this information. Perhaps one of our subordinate units conducting missions would be able to do something with this piece of data. But it does no one any good simply entered into a log or sitting in an inbox. Telling just one person can be the difference between victory and defeat. *Who else needs to know?*

I have encouraged my own team to post this on the top of their computer monitors. It is a good reminder that we need to constantly be reminded of the importance of sharing information.

As I think about times where I have really had my butt chewed (usually rightly so), it is for this shortcoming. I take action and fail to coordinate. I don't tell my partners, stakeholders, or higher head-quarters what I am doing—and it comes back to bite me. I fail to report, provide late or incomplete information, or miss a suspense without letting someone know—and it has the potential to cost my team the battle (or at least a couple of pounds off my backside).

- Having problems with a supplier? *Who else needs to know?*

- Not going to meet a quarterly goal? *Who else needs to know?*

- Getting ready to make a major announcement or move out on a bold initiative? *Who else needs to know?*

- Sitting on some bad news that may have impacts beyond just your project, or your little piece of the company? *Who else needs to know?*

Ensure people know your expectations for communication with you. Identify what you want to be told, when, how, etc. Any doubt will lead to misplaced assumptions about what you want to know. Post the "*WHO ELSE NEEDS TO KNOW?*" bumper sticker around the office to remind people of the importance of staying connected and sharing information.

Leaders must be clear about communication expectations. One way is to give teammates a standing set of reporting requirements (in the military we call it the Commander's Critical Information Requirements, or CCIR). This data is independent of the situation—a general set of "wake up the boss" information requirements. This list could range from things like death or serious injury to an employee or family member to significant financial or public relation issues (good or bad), or anything noteworthy that impacts on a major customer, account, or project milestone. CCIR should be published and reviewed periodically with subordinate leaders. When people know what is expected of them in this regard, they are infinitely more likely to stay engaged.

Communication is a two-way street. CCIR and similar information requirements are what we want from others. What do they want from us? Feedback, encouragement, and information that will enable their success. No matter the arena, people value the regular indicators of performance that lets them know that their work is valued and that they are doing the right thing. Success in execution then, is the by-product of software issues like performance counseling, feedback, on-the-spot recognition, and the sharing of lessons learned that enables the success of others.

Communication in Crisis

Sometimes things go wrong. We've all been there. At no point in the life of an organization or of a project is communication more important. People need to be confident that their reports, even when conveying bad news, are still encouraged.

Having been involved with any number of bad news situations myself, I have learned that nothing aggravates a critical situation (and perhaps itself contributes to creating crisis conditions) like people sitting on negative information. People have to know our information requirements, especially for difficult issues. Subordinates who are aware of our general expectations for notification will be more likely to meet them when the heat is on. In other words, if communication both ways is regular, then bad news is much easier to convey. Problems are not left on the table for others to deal with but shared early so that all can help reach appropriate solutions

I like to let people know that in crisis, I want to know the initial 5 "Ws"—who, what, where, when, why—as soon as possible, and that I will leave them alone to deal with the situation until they are available for a more detailed report. I try to be sure to emphasize that I am not interested in the blame game. I want to give them enough time to stop the bleeding, to allow them to move forward. In a crisis, blame and accountability must take a back seat to problem solving. I want people to talk to me with the full understanding that we are all on the same team.

After more than 25 years in the Army, I think I have finally learned to accept initial reports of "Contact . . . out," from my subordinates. This short communication burst is an abbreviated report of enemy contact. It's an indicator that my leaders are in crisis-management mode. This is not the time to demand detailed reports. I have learned that there is a way to deal with the situation without breathing down their necks and hindering their ability to win the fight. When they can give me more information, they will. And together we will resolve the crisis situation.

These are the three key components of communication in crisis situations that allow units to recover quickly, respond appropriately, and regain the momentum:

1. **Report immediately.** Don't overanalyze. Just state what you know, and let people trust that you will get back to them as soon as you have developed the situation. Keep communications short and simple.

2. **Include others in your decision making.** We should never try to figure everything out ourselves. Involving others in decision making, talking out various options, gives us the best chance of finding an appropriate solution. Leaders who take on all the burdens of decision making during times of crisis run the risk of missing alternatives that others might provide.

3. **Focus less on what happened and more on what you are going to do about it.** There will always be time to analyze the causes of crisis situations. That time is not when you are working on landing a plane in the Hudson River, as U.S. Airways pilot Chesley B. "Sully" Sullenberger learned in early 2009! Sully mentioned only once that he had lost his engines during takeoff due to a bird strike. No one pressed him for more information on how or why. Instead, the conversation focused on how to get the crisis under control.

Speak Like a Leader

If anything, our employees are likely to say they don't hear enough from their leader. I agree. Execution is usually impacted by a *lack* of communication, not from too much. I think there is so much more we can do to interact with our teammates:

- *Check in with key leaders and direct reports on a regular basis.* Be proactive and solicit feedback on how they are doing on their tasks or milestones, whether they have enough resources, etc. Call them, write them, or stop by. Keep your open door . . . open! Just checking in and being available to your team means everything.

- *Use every means available to maintain the "drumbeat" (priorities, shared vision, lessons learned, future plans, etc.).* This is where the hardware comes in with things like email, videos, blogs, podcasts, and social networking through the internet or organizational intranet. Just as important are less technologically intensive forums such as town hall meetings, brown bag lunches, and staff meetings. People have an intense desire to be connected to the mission and to their teammates. Our communication should enable this possibility.

- *Return emails.* Even a simple "OK . . . got it," means the world to people who want to know they are being heard.

- *Include people in decision-making.* Don't just tell people that their opinion counts without taking action on what they say. As discussed in Part I, including teammates in creating the shared vision will guarantee that they own the plans that they helped create!

Nothing misses the mark in conveying critical information like the dreaded "staff meeting." I have eliminated them in every organization in which I have served. My experience is that no one pays attention unless it is their turn to brief, and the entire focus is on the team leader. How can we spend so much time on a meeting that benefits only one person? My preference is to conduct Battlefield Update Briefings (BUBs), a communication forum that has greatly enhanced the situational awareness of each team on which I have served.

> *"The basic building block of good communications is the feeling that every human being is unique and of value."*
>
> ***Anonymous***

The BUB is designed to synchronize all of the activities of the unit with each other and within the framework of the unit mission and our shared vision. Everyone listens to ensure they understand the big picture of what is happening and that their activities are structured accordingly. The BUB can be fit anywhere within the week where it can best synchronize the activities of the entire team and generally take on the following framework:

- **Start with the big picture.** The operations staff usually begins by highlighting what is happening in the higher echelons, what units to the left and right are doing, and what key events have occurred since the last BUB. The lead intelligence officer identifies what the enemy (competition) is doing and gives his estimate for what might happen next. The goal is to create a common picture for the team, one in which everyone shares the same perspective of what is happening throughout the organization.

- **Review key metrics.** For a military unit, this may be the number of people and their location and disposition, status on key pieces of equipment, or progress toward key milestones. For a business unit, this may be financials (sales, revenue, overhead) or progress toward quarterly goals.

- **Synchronize.** BUBs serve as the forum to align ongoing subordinate actions. If the activities of one subordinate unit are in conflict with the overall unit purpose, or with another unit, they must be adjusted accordingly. All parties must leave the BUB with a full understanding of what is happening, what is important, and what they must do within the overall context of the team's mission.

- **Keep it short and focused.** Use a concise format—and stay with it. BUBs are not the forum for deep thinking or idle chatter. Get on with it.

- **Empower everyone to speak out if they have questions or if they sense a synchronization issue.** This is a session for the entire team, not just the leader. Create an environment in which the lowest-ranking trooper, who understands the big picture, can speak out if they believe something is wrong.

- **Close with a review of top priorities.** This is usually the opportunity for the leader to highlight what is important and what needs to happen to ensure synchronization of the team's efforts. It is also the best chance to inspire the team with a positive, mission-focused message that can motivate everyone to succeed.

Leader Business

Be clear about what words you use when you brief missions, issue orders and instructions, or talk about long range plans. An artilleryman can talk for hours on the difference between defeat and destroy. They each mean different things and have significantly different implications on the use of resources, time, and personnel. Don't say "*soon*" if you mean "*now*." Don't say "*should*" if you mean "*must*." Review priorities with your subordinates. Make it clear to all what is critical to you and what is just important.

Leaders must avoid the tendency to be "*info-maniacs*." Regularly examine your information requirements. If the reports from subordinates do not cause you to do anything, eliminate those reporting requirement. Your subordinates will thank you. Less is better.

Organizations and leaders who are consistently surprised by bad news must examine the culture that suppresses communication. Treating every member of the team with dignity and respect goes a long way toward opening up pockets of information within the organization. Leaders must cultivate a climate that values input, no matter the source; that welcomes criticism and bad news as opportunities for learning and growth; and that does not shoot the messenger. Such an organizational climate will empower subordinates to make suggestions, seek clarification, and communicate proactively—before crises develop.

Leaders are responsible for facilitating cross-talk within their organizations. Left to themselves, subordinates will rarely communicate outside of their respective stovepipes. Learning, accountability, situational awareness, execution—all are positive benefits from consistent cross-talk within high performing teams of teams.

Leaders must also be brutally honest with the truth. In the most difficult times, often all we have is our credibility. When people trust us, they will accept setbacks and difficult news, knowing that we are not spinning them and will communicate both positive and negative reports.

Effective communication demands leaders who care, who understand the needs of those whom they lead, and who can speak with courage and conviction. If we want people to listen, talk about what is important to them. Talk about how to be better, how to be more productive, and how we can help them succeed. Meet people where they are, physically and emotionally. That is the heart of effective communication.

Communication—before, during, and after the mission—is fundamental to victory in battle. More than just talking, real communication is a two-way dialogue that enables the successful execution of *good enough* plans. It is how positive, engaging, mission focused leaders, with the necessary communications hardware and software, connect people to purpose and accomplish the mission.

Marching Orders

- *Have you established your CCIR for your team? Do they clearly understand your communication requirements?*

- *What have you done lately to enable positive, proactive communication with your teammates?*

- *What will it take to turn your staff meeting into a BUB—something that adds value not just to you but to the productivity of the entire team?*

- *Do all of your information requirements, routine reports, etc. cause you to take action? If not, could they be eliminated?*

Chapter 13
Situational Awareness

"Situational awareness is a unique consciousness of one's
own immediate circumstances."
JOHN MICHAEL MAGNESS

Have you ever noticed how some people never seem surprised by anything? Good news: they expected it. Bad news: they saw it coming, and prepared accordingly. Unclear future? Not for these "visioneers." Inability to make decisions and execute the mission among the noise and chaos? Not these leaders.

Some people just have "it." I have known and worked with several leaders like this during my career. They always seemed to have their head in the game. They could monitor several different radio frequencies while simultaneously carrying on conversations with their teammates. They had whatever information they needed to make decisions right at their fingertips: maps, charts, summaries of key tasks and potential decision points for the day ahead. Oh, and they could manage all of this information at night . . . while sitting in the turret of a tank, navigating difficult terrain or city streets.

These warriors were always "plugged in," and nothing surprised them. They seemed to know everything about the enemy and about their own troops. They could make split-second decisions, seemingly based on only a single piece of information (but clearly with an understanding of the broader context of the situation), and appeared to think in a third dimension of which most can only dream. While their subordinates battled with the enemy to their front, these guys were thinking about the enemy to the flanks or even those that had yet to join the fight. It seemed to me that they were always thinking *not* about what would happen next, but what would occur after that.

Let's bring our discussion of *execution* to a close by considering the concept of situational awareness (SA). This is the ability to understand one's environment and to be able to make decisions and take actions—faster than anyone else—that impact not only current activities, but future operations as well. SA is the leader's ability to *see first*, to *understand first*, and to *act decisively* that keeps him one step ahead of his teammates, his peers, and his competition.

Pilots regularly refer to SA when discussing the skills necessary to fly a complex aircraft despite the apparent chaos of flight. In any operational context, great leaders have this ability. This is the awareness that *makes* things happen, that literally forces the action on favorable terms, and that carries the day in terms of mission accomplishment. Businessmen with SA get in—and out—of markets at the right time. They position themselves to be ready to deal with contingencies. They can handle diverse issues and complex situations with a steady hand and a reasoned mind. And like all the other responsibilities we have highlighted thus far, SA is an acquired skill that allows great leaders, like great pilots, to soar to the top.

See First

Good leaders practice what I call "scanning." Exposure to as many different sources of information provides the awareness of one's environment that facilitates timely and informed decisions. A military leader routinely "scans" his organization's command radio channel plus that of his higher headquarters. Business leaders scan by holding listening sessions within their own ranks. They interact with their employees to gauge first-hand the morale, workload, and capabilities of their team.

I have found that exposure to diverse information streams provides an understanding of my situation. Scanning a wide variety of media sources (books, magazines, websites, or newsletters) provides context and fresh ideas. Industry conferences and seminars offer best practices and emerging technologies. Sitting in on meetings with my boss (or my leaders two or more levels up) helps provide an understanding of the challenges and opportunities for which they might need my help.

My brother, John Magness, is a businessman in Southern California. Before that, he was a helicopter pilot, flying combat missions in Desert Storm, Somalia, and Haiti. He and I have discussed this concept of SA from the perspective of a military aviator and its importance to *execution* (a topic which he highlights in his own book, *Pilot Vision*). Pilots are always scanning—quick glances at the gauges, at the radar screen, out the window, back to the gauges—to assess the status of the plane and the surrounding environment, and to provide indicators of whether the mission is on track.

While there are hundreds, perhaps thousands of pieces of data that pilots might like to monitor, there are only gauges for a few key indicators on the pilot's "head-up display." Consider these approaches to scanning from the aviation community and how we might relate them to what it takes to have good SA in our own *ground-based* operations:

- *Altitude indicator.* Am I flying at the right elevation?

- *Heading and speed indicator.* Am I traveling in a direction and at a pace that will get me to my destination?

- *Attitude indicator.* Is my plane flying level?

- *Fuel gauge.* Am I resourced sufficiently for my mission?

- *Radar.* Who else is operating in my area?

Establishing these types of gauges will help us maintain situational awareness in our respective cockpits. What information must we have at our fingertips—our own "head-up displays"—to make informed decisions? Identify specific information requirements that we must have in our notebook or on our computer desktop and ensure everyone knows what they are. They have to become the sort of basic indices that we scan and review regularly with our teammates.

A leader never has all the information he or she wants. Those who practice scanning, and whose "head-up displays" provide them with real-time indicators of progress, focus their communication in ways that fill in the gaps. Their meetings, counseling, performance reviews, and small-talk around the office, help them "see first."

> *"I don't skate to where the puck is. I skate to where the puck is going to be."*
>
> **Wayne Gretsky**

What information is important for "seeing first?" Start with anything that impacts milestones or task execution. Talk about your critical information requirements (CCIR). Check issues regarding your BFT (resources, alignment, etc.). Review any changes to your assumptions about strengths, weaknesses, opportunities, or threats (SWOT). Leaders scan through these indicators regularly to sense important changes or potential decision points.

Seeing *first* means doing all of this more efficiently than others. Some of this comes from practice, some is enabled by technology, and some is the result of simply ensuring that people are talking about those things that contribute to mission accomplishment. Leaders facilitate good cross-talk among subordinate business units. They share lessons learned with the team. They promote the understanding that information is valued . . . and that speed of delivery matters.

Understand First

Most discussions about SA begin and end with "seeing first." Practice scanning, have the right gauges on your display, and focus your communication—that should be enough, right? Well, true SA goes to the next level. It requires an understanding of how each piece of new information fits into the "big picture." Situational *understanding* requires constant analysis, deliberate thought, and examination of questions like these:

- *What does this raw data mean?*

- *Where does this new information fit into my understanding of the past, present, and future?*

- *Who else needs to know? Who can confirm the possible meaning of this new information?*

- *How does this information impact my organization?*

- *How will it impact my competitors?*

- *What happens next—and what do we need to do about it?*

Do you have this level of situational understanding? Isn't this what differentiates the good leaders from the great, always keeping one step ahead of the competition? We can't be content just to *see* first. We have to continuously update our awareness of our environment in order to truly *understand* first.

I participated in the Army's first digital exercises in the late 90s as a member of the 4th Infantry Division at Fort Hood, Texas. I trained a number of those same units when they later deployed out to the NTC in 2001. I witnessed the power of having the ability to "*see first*" using networks and new operational procedures that leveraged the technological enablers that went all the way down to the individual soldier level. It was great to have all the shared data.

It was a challenge for many to make the leap to *situational understanding*. We all had to recognize that the machines worked for us, and not the other way around. We had to overcome the fact that the raw data was simply overwhelming if we didn't apply the sort of "old school" analysis that has always enabled decision making.

Doing so made SA a combat multiplier, and those digital units could out-execute anything that had been seen on the battlefield before.

The key enabler to execution in this sort of environment is what is called a Common Operating Picture (COP). This is the assembled data—synthesized, analyzed, and shared with the full team—which allows all leaders to see the battlefield the same way, a *common* picture. They can see the location of all of their teammates, where they are in relation to each of them, and query various databases to assess resources or pull up recent reports.

The COP also reflects known enemy positions, making it easier to move to positions of advantage. With this sort of shared perspective combined with people communicating proactively about changes and new information and collaborating about future actions, the synergy was truly lethal. Decision cycles were shortened. Leaders were significantly better informed. Mutual trust among teammates was certain.

It is this ability to see and understand that enables bold, decisive actions. It is no different in business. Databases need to be linked together. Management tools, like a COP, have to highlight issues in performance and opportunities to seize an advantage. In any setting, the key is not the computer—but the operator. People have to want to communicate, to share critical information, to translate raw data into actionable intelligence. Leaders have to facilitate the growth that makes the picture of what *is* help people understand what's coming next. It is not enough to simply *see* what is happening without translating it, answering the "so what?" question, and being ready to do something about it.

Act Decisively

Without action, seeing and understanding first is irrelevant. One can *see* the lights of an approaching truck, be *aware* that they could get hurt, and still get run over. Leaders must be capable of operating quickly and decisively based on higher levels of situational awareness. They must be able to seize the initiative based on small pieces of information that fit within the leader's perception of the past, present, and future. True SA demands action. This is where leaders deliver.

This truly is a discriminator in assessing leaders, isn't it? The great leaders are the ones who take bold action, who can sort through the chaos and make good decisions, whose intuition about future activities seems almost prophetic. It is not magic—it's SA. And as I indicated previously, it is an acquired skill.

Isn't it easier to make decisions and take action in chaos, with limited information, if you have been there before? Leaders must always be ready to say "yes" to opportunities to broaden our knowledge base. New positions and duties, and increased leadership responsibilities, further expand our experience levels. We should be thinking the same way about our teammates. Providing them with these sorts of growth opportunities makes them more likely to take action when the time comes.

As we discussed in Part II, short of actual experience, nothing prepares leaders to take action like practice. Similar to athletes preparing for competition, we need to place ourselves and our field leaders in "game" situations to develop the sort of muscle density that is ready to spring into action. Sometimes this can be an individual exercise such as the review of a case study and thinking through possible solutions, or a more deliberate drill conducted as a group. Execution is made possible when our SA drills get us to the following:

- Understand the positioning of our teammates. Where will they be and what will they be doing if we need them? How can I help them and what can they do for me?

- Focus less on what we will *do* and more on what we will *decide* and when we will *decide* it. Determine the information requirements that will enable our decisions. Who will provide us the necessary information and where will they be when we need it? What will our gauges read when we have to pull the trigger?

- Where will our competitors be and what might they be doing that will require action from our team? How will we know when they are doing it? Who will report it?

- Think about contingencies and branch plans to determine second, third, and fourth order effects. Identify cause and effect from each anticipated action. How do we position our team to take advantage of potential outcomes?

Practice Battlefield Circulation

Combat leaders cannot have good SA without regularly moving to a vantage point with a clear view of the battlefield, close enough to gauge the sights and sounds of warfare, talking to subordinate leaders and their soldiers, looking them in the eye, finding out—first hand—the answers to questions such as: Do they understand the plan? Do they have what they need to be successful? Do they understand their opponent? Are they confident in themselves and in their leaders? These are personal observations that cannot be gained from a PowerPoint presentation, in a conference call, or in an email.

You may have heard of it referred to as "management by walking around." In military terms it is called "battlefield circulation." It is that essential leadership activity of getting out from behind the desk and strengthening your SA by being in the field and engaging those who do the work, who generate the ideas, and who execute our best laid plans and strategies.

In business, battlefield circulation means getting down to the shop floor, talking to the maintenance and production crews. It demands that leaders devote quality time in the field with the sales staff; interact with the men and women in research and development (R&D); see what the marketing folks are up to; meet subordinate leaders in *their* cubicles; and talk to customers. Get out there!

My brigade commander in the 4th Infantry Division, then-Colonel Rick Lynch, was the best I've seen at battlefield circulation. He entered his headquarters early in the morning for an update on the current operations and the events of the evening. Each subordinate staff representative briefed him until he had a complete understanding of the friendly and enemy situation. He then spent an hour or so with his planning staff, discussing future operations, at his level about 48-72 hours in the future. He gave them guidance on how he wanted to fight the next battle and how he envisioned the battle after that, outlining very clearly his vision, his intent, and specific tasks that he expected to be completed prior to his return.

With that complete, he was free to circulate. He moved from subordinate unit to subordinate unit, talking to leaders one and two levels below his and spot-checking with the privates and sergeants down where the rubber met the road: *How was the current battle going? Do you have all the troops and equipment you need to be successful? What do you think about the plans for the next battle? Do you understand the big picture and how your unit's success contributes to the overall organization vision? Have you heard about the successes and failures in the unit on your flank? How can you apply their lessons learned? Do you have any heroes I can personally recognize for their contribution while I am here?* (Keep in mind, this was the 4th ID, that great digital unit with all of those cutting-edge technological tools. Lynch knew he couldn't get this sort of feedback from a videoconference or from icons on a computer monitor. He had to be down on the ground to get these answers.)

> *"The leader goes where he can best influence the battle, where his moral and physical presence can be felt, and where his will to achieve victory can best be expressed, understood, and acted upon."*
>
> **Army Field Manual 100-5**

When Lynch was done, and before he moved to another unit, he would call back to his headquarters: *Any updates? Here is what I learned from this unit—please share this information with the staff. This is the feedback I got from my leaders about future operations and how I think we should modify our plans to include their recommendations. Do you have anything for me? OK, got it. I'm moving to the next unit.*

Battlefield circulation is the key to effective SA. It is regular movement throughout one's area of responsibility designed to enhance the SA of the leader and those he or she leads. It is not random visits but rather a well-planned, disciplined travel and meeting schedule that positions the leader, in the right place and at the right time, to influence the battle. It should be scheduled and designed to accomplish the following:

- **Meet people on their "turf."** Assess subordinate performance and identify emerging leaders. Conduct performance counseling. Determine for yourself if projects are being completed on time, and on budget. Assess working conditions first-hand. Determine whether team members have the tools to do what is asked of them.

- **Sit down with key customers.** Take some time, if you have not already, to put together a list of current and prospective customers and include them in your circulation pattern: When did you last meet with them? Are you meeting their needs? Are they thrilled with your product and your performance? In business, key "customers" may also include board members or major shareholders. In education, a school principal may target a handful of influential students representing the demographics of the student body.

- **Spend some time with the lowest private, the new team member, and the rank-and-file workers.** How is their morale? Do they have what they need to do their jobs? Ask the line workers for feedback on your "great ideas." Few will hesitate to tell you exactly what they think. Do they understand your vision? Gauge for yourself how communication flows in your organization—ask the new employees what they know about where you are headed organizationally in-both the short and long term.

The bottom line here is that we must get out of our offices, get out of our comfort zone, and be where the troops are to have effective SA. Whether meeting with field staff or key customers, battlefield circulation is our chance to listen and make observations about the team's readiness and ability to accomplish the mission. This is how we can *see* and *understand* first, and be ready to *act* decisively. This skill is the essential leader responsibility that puts us in position to immediately solve problems, seize opportunities, and accomplish the mission—on any battlefield.

Leader Business

Leaders with high SA must conduct what is called a *running estimate,* a continuous analysis that considers the meaning of each new piece of information. This constant update and reassessment enables the anticipation of potential decisions based on an ongoing examination of three factors (which we first encountered in our initial mission analysis):

1. *See yourself.* What is the implication of our collective strengths and weaknesses?

2. *See the enemy.* What is my competition doing that imperils my organization and its success? What challenges can I anticipate? What other issues hinder execution and the attainment of our goals?

3. *See the terrain.* What is the nature of the current and future operational climate? How do "terrain" issues such as fuel and other raw material price fluctuations, inflation, regulatory issues, current events, and the labor pool impact on our organization and on our future decision making?

Bold action based on limited information requires confident leaders with internal compasses—a kind of a "*spider-sense*" for leaders, if you are familiar with the web-slinging superhero. Leaders must develop and be guided by an "inner voice" that can make sense of chaos. I can't count the number of times I have failed because I have neglected to listen to my gut or to trust my instincts. My SA was high. I have either been afraid to act, *over*-confident in my abilities, or just plain dumb. Often it has been all three.

Our spider-sense should be tingling when we don't monitor our health. We can't take battlefield circulation to the extreme. If we are always on the road and never sleeping in our own bed—watch out. We have to maintain balance between time in the office and out walking around. Leaders keep a pulse on their physical, mental, spiritual, and family health. Many are the potholes that threaten the "road warrior" doing well intended travel across the battlefield. Let's commit to be where we need to be, when we need to be there, to influence key events and subordinate leaders and to enhance our own SA—but also to keep it in balance.

Great leaders see and understand their environment, know where they are going (as if they had already been there), and take action. SA is not the unique domain for aviators or military leaders. Like most other leadership traits, it results from repetition, experience, hard work, battle hardening, and desire. If we want to be execution warriors, to separate ourselves from our competition, we have to have this high level of SA, and be ready to take action. Have no doubt—if we are out there with our troops, being where we need to be to influence the battle, we won't need to look for opportunities to demonstrate the importance of this skill. Those opportunities will find us.

Marching Orders

* *Have you established your COP for your team? Do you all have a shared vision of what is happening in mission execution?*

- *How might you enhance your personal situational awareness? What 5-7 personal information items do you want at your fingertips to enhance your decision making?*

- *Are you getting out from behind your desk and circulating the battlefield? What do you need to do to be able to spend more time where the action is?*

PART IV

LEARN

Chapter 14

Leaders Learn

"We don't learn from experience.
We learn from reflecting on experience."
JOHN DEWEY

As the Army emerged from the Vietnam War, it found itself in a strategically precarious position. The demands of nearly a decade of conflict had drained the service's resources, leaving it organizationally exhausted. Meanwhile, its Cold War competition (the Red Army) had reached a position of technological parity *and* numerical superiority. Military leaders struggled to develop strategies that would strengthen the force and prepare it for success in future battles.

To borrow from author Spencer Johnson, the Army discovered that someone had "moved their cheese." While they were off doing something else, their main competitors had become a stronger, more advanced foe. The likely site of future conflict was not going to be the jungles of Southeast Asia but the rolling plains of Europe, the deserts and rocky soils of the Middle East, and the complex terrain of the Korean Peninsula. Doctrine, training methods, and equipment were outdated and increasingly irrelevant. The post-Vietnam Army was clearly a mess. The game had changed and, sadly, adaptability was not among the Army's strengths.

Fortunately, in the late 1970s the Army embraced the concept of learning. Its leaders studied the lessons of other wars for possible implications on fighting and winning against a superior force. It adopted performance-oriented training, a concept whereby soldiers were trained to a defined standard, not just based on training hours completed. It developed new doctrinal systems and responsive organizations that could fight and win the first battle of the next war. It developed and procured technologies that enabled its more offensive-minded tactics. Training systems incorporated all of these lessons and provided advanced instruction to new recruits and leaders.

From all of this was born the second "Happiest Place on Earth," (yes, trailing only Disneyland!) the National Training Center at Fort Irwin. In a remote area of the beautiful Mojave Desert, training evolved to focus on standards and more rigorous evaluations in order to improve units and their leaders. Learning was reinforced through the deliberate examination of unit performance, or After Action Reviews (AARs), which forced leaders to improve, both personally and professionally.

In two tours of duty at the NTC nearly 20 years later, my role was to enable this type of learning while serving as Observer/Controller, or OC. I was the equivalent of a professional coach or mentor to training unit leaders. Equally important, I was an accountability partner, helping my counterparts understand the standard and where they could improve. This was the approach I used in my AARs, built upon the belief that learning requires brutal honesty and the disciplined sharing of best practices. I believe that it is largely through this philosophy that our military has established a culture of learning and professional growth. Hopefully, the guys I trained would validate the effectiveness of these methods!

To be honest, I found the life of an OC to be a lot like being a cowboy. I rode around all day on my trusty steed (my Humvee), dressed in the latest western (military) gear, and kept the herd (the training unit) in line. If they strayed, I gently pointed them in the right direction until they reached their destination.

We had our own brand (the "Sidewinders"), a distinctively rugged appearance (we wore dark sunglasses and never took our helmets off), and knew the terrain like the backs of our sun-baked hands. At night, we pulled away from the herd (still close enough to know if they were getting into trouble), lit a fire, and enjoyed a nice steak and some good stories in the company of friends.

It was a hard life, week after week in the harsh Mojave Desert. Yet it was the most professionally rewarding experience of my career. The learning never stopped. Each event yielded a different set of lessons which I could review with the unit leaders, or share with the Army through its various professional publications. I collected best practices and passed them along from one warrior to the next. Day after day, mission after mission, we kept up this disciplined approach of raising the bar for unit—and leader—performance.

> *"Failure is in a sense the highway to success, as each discovery of what is false leads us to seek earnestly after what is true."*
>
> **John Keats**

Without question, as has been the case since its first training rotation in 1981, the NTC is the Army's most intense learning environment, both for training units and for those of us who had the great fortune of serving as OCs. One cannot help but grow in this ultimate leadership laboratory. It reflects our military's commitment to continuous improvement, to training every single member of the combat team, and to ensuring that it can remain without peer on the battlefield. Coaching, teaching, training, and continuous improvement through AARs—these are the means by which leaders, and the organizations they serve, learn and grow within the *Leader Business* cycle.

Leaders Learn

Part IV of *Leader Business* focuses on the means by which effective leaders get on top and stay there: they learn. Good leaders understand that they must always be growing. They must always be seeking new sources of data about performance, customers, technology, emerging opportunities, and the marketplace. They have a hunger for information, the enhanced situational awareness that we highlighted in Part

III, and a passion for knowledge that they infuse in those they lead.

Leaders learn by investing in every single member of the team, no matter their rank or position. They create the belief that no one is more or less important than anyone else, an attitude that permeates the culture, creating conditions of empowerment, confidence, and mutual trust. This is the type of growth that feeds on itself. People feel like they matter and they perform better. Good performance generates lessons that are shared across the team. The rising tide of learning lifts all boats . . . and the people who crew them.

Let's begin this final part of *Leader Business* with a discussion about AARs. These are the post-mission debriefs that address what went well, and should be integrated into future operations, and what went poorly, and must be improved. Done correctly, they are rank-less, ego-less sessions in which the team focuses totally and completely on job #1: the mission. Everyone benefits and no one is left behind. Good ideas are vetted and shared. Teammates are held accountable for their actions and commit to specific improvements. The unwavering embrace of AARs is a key element of the path to sustained greatness.

I led many post-mission AARs at the NTC and I am passionate about the value they add to individual growth and team performance. Conducted out in the field in high-tech trailers, on the hood of a Humvee, or one-on-one during the dreaded "walk in the desert" (as in *"Hey, leader, let's take a walk"*), AARs functioned as learning accelerators.

Leaders with a willingness to be open to criticism and self-examination, who readily accept coaching and feedback, demonstrate continuous growth. Warriors with a similar goal—to be the best they can possibly be—push each other to improve. Every member of the team gets feedback. This is what learning looks like. Is this a perfect world? You bet. As much as 115-degree heat, 72 hours without sleep, cold food, and an enemy who seems to be inside your decision cycle can constitute a perfect world. But it was most definitely an environment ripe for learning!

Learning: Our Best ROI

Obviously, AARs are not the only way that people learn. More traditionally, they benefit from investments in various means of training. Leaders balance the need for mission accomplishment with the growth and development that prepares people for future requirements. Effective leaders focus out, serving as coaches and mentors for the teams they lead, with a keen awareness of the needs of those they serve. Learning is an investment in excellence, with real costs and measurable benefits, by leaders who truly, passionately care about their teammates.

Learning does not necessarily have to be a major expense. Sometimes it is as simple as one-on-one counseling of subordinates or the sharing of best practices and new ideas over lunch. It can occur in the oft-emphasized but rarely implemented practice of measuring performance and potential in formal and informal counseling. The key point is that learning is continuous and that every person on the team, from the school superintendent, to the principal, to the teacher, and to the janitor benefits from some balanced level of investment. It is the leader's responsibility to make this happen.

Make no mistake, it *is* an investment. In *Fortune* magazine's regular listing of the "100 Best Companies to Work For," the top organizations provide 80-100 hours of annual training. Why are companies like Google, Whole Foods Market, and The Container Store such coveted employment sites? No doubt because professional training is among the benefits that help attract and retain the talent that makes these companies successful. Interestingly, the top companies' average investment in training is less than 1% of revenue. This small but continuous investment can mean everything to those who join our companies. We better believe it means the world to those who stay.

In Los Angeles with the Army Corps of Engineers, we made a deliberate effort to make training a priority. We established formal leader development and mentorship programs. We doubled our training budget. We put an emphasis on professional competency and increased our cadre of credentialed Project Managers (PMPs) by 400%.

When I saw how important the element of sustainability would be in new construction, I challenged my team to pursue accreditation in LEED (Leadership in Energy and Environmental Design). At least a dozen employees joined me in passing this exam (no doubt because they didn't want the Colonel showing them up!).

Even as a federal agency, I wanted us to be recognized as a "Best Company to Work For." To me, the question was not, "how could we afford it?" but rather, "how could we afford *not* to?" If we wanted to be able to attract new talent, retain the great people we already had, and remain competitive and efficient in the eyes of our customers, we had to put a priority on being a learning organization. We had to make learning part of our culture and a mandatory component of the project delivery process. People, processes, teams and their leaders all had to improve or we would lose talent, market share, and our well-deserved reputation for excellence. Remember that expression *"Mission first, people always?"* Leadership is not an either/or proposition. We must do both.

Cheers for the Failures

I have come to believe that if we want to find a great leader, look for the colossal failures. They are the ones who have reached high and gone after the big prize. Too many people are satisfied with mediocrity. A few great warriors are still out there. They are the bold, innovative risk-takers who recognize that true learning occurs when we stretch—personally and professionally—and put ourselves in the arena to face the lions. Sometimes, the lions win. But I salute those with the *cajones* to try . . . even if they lose the occasional limb!

There's a well-known military anecdote about a young, fresh-faced lieutenant who once approached a grizzled colonel to seek his advice about how to be a good leader. The colonel's simple advice: "Make good decisions." While the lieutenant appreciated the candid feedback, he probed deeper, seeking more specific insights on how to make good decisions. The colonel's response: "Experience." Clearly frustrated, the newly commissioned officer stated that his lack of experience was what led him to seek out this seasoned officer's counsel. "How do I get the experience I will need to be a decisive leader?" The colonel's terse reply said it all: "Bad decisions!"

I don't doubt the truth of this vignette. We learn more from failure and bad decisions than when everything goes smoothly. Failure is the incentive to "buckle our chinstrap" a little tighter, to apply ourselves a little more diligently to avoid future setbacks. This is the growth cycle we have to foster in our own lives and in the organizations that we lead:

Aim high >> Fail occasionally and capture lessons learned >> Focus on how to improve >> Learn and get better >> Aim higher!

This continues to be what I look for in potential leaders for my own team. At every hiring interview, I always ask, *"What is your greatest failure, and what did you learn from it?"* First, I want people to be able to recite their failures. I want them to demonstrate to me that they don't play it conservatively, that they are willing to push the envelope. I don't want them to have to strain to remember them because the bitter taste of defeat is still burned into their memory.

Secondly, I want them to convince me that they learned from the event. I want to hear about growth, development, applied training, and their subsequent successes. Give me risk-taking, ambitious, energetic warriors with their share of failures any day. A core group like that can change a culture. A team of failures, who help each other get up off the ground, dust themselves off, and get back in the fight—better and stronger from the lessons they have learned—can change the world.

Connect the Dots

The most challenging class I ever took was a wastewater treatment course at the University of Texas taught by Dr. Desmond F. Lawler. He wore me out during my first semester of graduate studies, where I truly found the limits of my mental capacity. Man, do I ever hate differential equations! Yet, I have no doubt that these battle scars have enhanced my learning ever since.

Perhaps the greatest lesson I learned from Dr. Lawler was when he shared his philosophy about students who desired to audit his course. You see, the line was quite long for those who wished to learn from this award-winning teacher, but wanted to do so without receiving a grade. Dr. Lawler's policy was that anyone who wished to audit was welcome to do so. But they would still have to attend every class, participate in each lecture, do all the homework, and take all the tests. That shortened the line quickly! In his mind, anything less was a waste of time for both him and the auditing student. It was only through this level of full participation that the ideas he was sharing would make any sense.

> *"We get the leaders we create."*
>
> **Peter Block**

As contradictory as this seemed at the time (to do all the work without earning a grade is a tough pill to swallow), Dr. Lawler was right. I feel the same way about those who think they can audit through life, stop pursuing excellence, stop growing, and become set in their ways. Auditing—failing to learn, to find new ways to improve, to connect the dots in ways that solve problems and make sense of the world around us—leads to complacency. Complacency—in graduate school, business, or combat leads to wasted time and irrelevance.

Most people emphasize the urgent, focusing on crisis after crisis, while neglecting the things, like learning, that help secure a sustainable future. Great leaders take the time to think, to look over the horizon, and to learn about their profession. They train and get trained, a never-ending commitment to growth and improvement. They coach others while seeking their own mentors who can provide context and perspective to their issues and experiences. Great leaders connect the dots, both personally and for the teams they lead.

Spiral Development

Frankly, I considered making this discussion of learning the opening section of *Leader Business*. Good *planning* must begin with an understanding of what has already occurred through the incorporation of best practices and lessons learned. Similarly, *preparation* and *execution* are fueled by learning and the feedback that helps improve both. Learning shapes every facet of our business operation and every one of our responsibilities within the *Leader Business* cycle.

Think of it this way: Remember the standard for our plans? *Good enough* gets us out the gate. But continuous *learning* and feedback provides new information that enables refinements to our plan and adjustments to our preparation tasks. Organizations are always being re-aligned based on best practices or the incorporation of new technologies. AARs and feedback from coaches yield new processes and procedures that feed back into our *planning*, *preparation*, and *execution*. It is what I call spiral development: keep learning, keep developing, and keep getting better.

I saw this sort of spiral development while serving with the "Digital Brigade" at Fort Hood, Texas. At the time, we were provided every imaginable new technology (one of my leaders called them all *fish finders*) for inclusion in the suite of capabilities that our unit would test. Some were great. Others added no value. After each test, we provided feedback to focused data collectors about our likes/dislikes and suggested improvements. Developers added a new patch, feature, or toggle switch and came back with something that hopefully satisfied our warfighting and information management requirements. Equipment operators shared lessons learned and found new ways of incorporating all of these new gadgets.

This is the learning cycle we all must cultivate within our organizations. Facilitated by the leader, constant dialogue about good ideas, emerging technologies, and best practices keeps everyone's head in the game. The two-way street of feedback (yes, it does go both ways) provides input that helps everyone grow. Adjustments are made every day to our plans, to the alignment of our resources, and to the techniques we employ to accomplish our respective tasks.

Leaders adjust their styles to meet the ever-changing demands of the mission. Those who commit to learning never get bored, rarely repeat mistakes, and find energy in the excitement of each new challenge. I love this stuff!

Leader Business

As we have highlighted in so many other areas, the best ideas often come from the trenches, from the men and women who are closest to the problem. We learn the most when we listen to others. Keeping our doors—and our ears—open provides the learning opportunities that become best practices and meaningful initiatives. Continuous scanning of inputs from employees, customers, competitors, and industry leaders gives us the sort of new ideas that help maintain relevancy in our markets.

Continuous learning must be focused both outward and inward. We want to know what is happening in the world around us and to have the sort of situational awareness that we described in Part III. We get this through participation at conferences, trade associations, and industry gatherings. We similarly need to be aware of our strengths and weaknesses and be constantly monitoring our own growth and development. Personality tests, strength assessments, and feedback from mentors can help us understand how we process information, where we can improve, and what we need to do to become more effective leaders.

Successful leaders understand the importance of continuing to read and write. Reading offers opportunities to leverage a diverse range of opinions and practices that can be used to propel future growth. Even reading for pleasure provides a measure of intellectual sharpening and exposure to ideas that help broaden one's leadership base.

Putting ideas to paper forces us to connect the dots and to understand, at a much deeper level, what we believe—and why. Professional writing is a mechanism, practiced by capable leaders at every level, which allows us to make sense of the world around us. It also serves as a means to develop others who might benefit from our perspectives. Effective leaders know that the more they write, the better writers they become. And by putting their ideas in the arena of public discourse, they enhance the collective wisdom of their respective personal and professional communities.

Good leaders ensure that every employee has an Individual Development Plan (IDP). This is a road map that charts a plan for growth to help our teammates see where they are going. It demonstrates a commitment to learning and a readiness to invest in each person. Looking out 3-5 years helps align resources and give some predictability to employees and the organization such that the impacts of future training and developmental assignments can be minimized, and the benefits of both can be maximized.

Learning never stops. Winning teams continue to evolve. I told you about the Army's transformation after Vietnam. Fast forward to 2001, another critical time for the service and for our nation. Once again, the Army measured itself and came up short. The cheese had moved. The organization built to fight the Soviets now had to deal with simultaneous wars, terrorists, roadside bombs, urban operations, and completely foreign cultures. Once again, the Army went into a cycle of learning, developing new systems, equipment, doctrine, and tactics for evolving requirements in the Middle East. Change is constant. The best never rest.

When it comes to learning, we have to change or be changed. Organizations that do not commit to learning risk irrelevancy in their respective battlefields. Processes and procedures become outdated. People do things simply because they have always done so. Employees and their leaders lack inspiration, motivation, and energy. Great leaders invest in learning, staying ahead of trends, bringing new skills to problem solving and decision making, and sustaining the sort of passionate, exciting workplaces that both customers and employees seek.

The cheese will move. Leaders who learn will not only move with it, they will position themselves and the organizations they lead to take over the whole cheese-production and distribution system.

Like the military that emerged from Vietnam or 9-11, they become learning organizations that dominate their opposition. That makes learning . . . *Leader Business*.

Marching Orders

- *How are you investing in the learning of every single member of your team?*

- *Do you have a system for rigorously examining performance in a rank-less, no-holds barred approach?*

- *How do you capture and disseminate best practices?*

- *What was your greatest failure—and what did you learn from it?*

Chapter 15
Peeling Back the Onion

"Remember the two benefits of failure. First, if you do fail, you learn what doesn't work; and second, failure gives you the opportunity to try a new approach."
ROGER VON OECH

Following Operation Desert Storm in 1991, I was one of hundreds of thousands of soldiers who, within hours of the cease-fire, were already tasked with examining the lessons of the battle. Despite the obvious success demonstrated in fighting and winning a 100-hour war, our focus was on what had not gone well. There was no back-slapping and little talk about how great a team we had assembled. We wanted to identify ways that the world's best fighting force could improve.

The lessons learned in 1991 were clearly evident a dozen years later during Operation Iraqi Freedom. Improvements in navigation technology, communication equipment, night vision capabilities, better friend/foe discernment tools, smart munitions, unmanned aerial vehicles, and the "fish finders" I was training with in those digital exercises in the late 90s were all based around the lessons of the previous war. Army doctrine, training, and leader development were similarly adapted to reflect the lessons of that war. We identified our shortcomings, made changes, and continued to improve. And remember, all of this change occurred after we *won* a war in 100 hours!

There is no question of our Army's prowess on the battlefield. Despite the complexities and challenges of current operations in Iraq and Afghanistan, there is little doubt that they are still the best in the world. They are well led, well trained, well-equipped—probably the best fighting force ever assembled.

We know of their success on the battlefield and their reputation both as peacemakers and peacekeepers. But no greater accolade can be granted to the Army than that of *learning* organization. Its commitment to continuous improvement, to analyzing and learning from mistakes, and to taking corrective action help ensure that the Army will remain unchallenged as the world's best.

So what does it take for an organization at the top of its game to continue to improve? What kinds of meaningful investments in learning help identify and share best practices? What systems contribute to the ability to sustain excellence? These are the issues that, like the Army, every one of the teams we lead must address. In the answer to these questions lies another key component of the business of leaders: leaders learn. How we do so in the Army is classified. (OK, not really!) But I am breaking it down for you here in order to provide a framework for organizational and personal improvement, ensuring continued dominance for your team—in any arena.

Let me pose one more question: Does your team have a mechanism to honestly assess mission completion in a routine way that provides the sort of feedback that we all need to grow? If you say yes, then when was your last session? If you can't remember (don't worry—you are not alone) then perhaps you might want to consider the Army's approach to learning.

Good to Great author Jim Collins refers to them as "autopsies without blame." Athletic coaches call them post-game film sessions, or the "game after the game." Others call them debriefs, huddles, or close-outs. In the Army they are know as After Action Reviews, or AARs. Army warriors and leaders swear by them as the single most effective approach to continuous improvement. The Army may not have invented the concept, but it clearly has mastered the execution.

Put simply, AARs are no-holds-barred reviews of what happened and why. They capture what went well (and should be sustained) and what did not go well (and should be improved). They are rank-less, burtally honest accountability sessions that help lead to continuous improvement. Best practices are identified and shared. Shortcomings are identified and corrected on the spot.

When used correctly, the AAR is a beautiful thing to behold. I know of no better mechanism for promoting growth in a team. Conducted promptly (immediately after mission, milestone, or activity completion), it allows lessons to be learned and applied directly to our operations. It initially took the military a little time to make AARs part of its routine business processes, but now you can see them being done, at all levels of the organization, every single day. AARs are the centerpiece of the Army's approach to learning, and an important part of the business of leaders.

After Action Reviews

I talk a lot about failure. I like to celebrate those who lose, yet are not defeated. I am inspired by those who fall, pick themselves up, and grow stronger. I believe it is important that we each push ourselves, take on more and more risk, and experience life (personally and professionally) out on the edge. In doing so, sometimes we will fail. But what we learn from these failures is what defines us, what propels us to even greater heights. Learning from failure is the key to the growth and development of any leader. Establishing a culture of learning within the teams we lead is a critical management responsibility.

I have tried to teach this early to my youngest daughter, who learned her own lessons about failure last year. She put herself in the arena and ran a great campaign for her middle school's vice presidency. She worked hard for weeks on her campaign and gave a great speech in front of the entire school. Despite her efforts, she lost. Heartbreaking for her, and pretty rough on campaign manager Dad.

So we held a family AAR and talked about failure. We discussed the failures of Abraham Lincoln. We pondered the implications of a man who ran for state legislature and lost; who ran for Congress and was defeated; who unsuccessfully ran for the U.S. Senate not once but twice. We talked about a man who lost plenty of elections before being ultimately elected to the Presidency in 1860.

More importantly, we talked about learning from our failures. We discussed how each time Lincoln failed, he jumped right back into the arena and found a way to keep advancing. When Lincoln was defeated for nomination for Congress in 1843, he established his own law practice and ultimately was elected in 1846. When he was defeated for U.S. Senator in 1854, he turned around and got elected to the Illinois state legislature. Lincoln never quit, never stopped advancing, kept learning, and took two steps forward for every step backward.

My daughter hopefully learned this lesson early in her life— that it is not what happens to us that defines who we are, but rather how we respond to it. As with Lincoln, I encouraged my daughter to not give up. If she could not serve as VP, she could still be a part of the student council. She could stay engaged and continue to be an active part of the school leadership team. She could keep her head up, congratulate her opponent, and demonstrate to the school that she is a person of character, even when things don't go her way.

> *"Change is only another word for learning. Therefore, the theories of learning will also be the theories of changing. If you want to change, try learning, one might say, or more precisely, if you want to be more in control of your change, take learning more seriously."*
>
> ***Charles Handy***

Our AAR focused on where we both could improve. We agreed there were things that she (we!) could have done better. She was not aggressive enough in getting her campaign material together. She did not read the demographics of the school well enough and failed to build the coalitions she needed to win. Learning can be so powerful when we open ourselves to honest assessment and focused criticism.

While it was hard for a middle schooler to engage in this type of self-examination, I believe that these are lessons she can apply if and when she runs for office again—and I am confident she will!

Let's examine in detail the elements of an effective After Action Review. Basically, you need a disciplined, systematic approach to gathering lessons learned and holding units and individuals accountable for meeting objectives. These reviews can be led by the unit leader, a trained outside facilitator, or by any other capable consensus builder available for this critical task. They should be rankless, fully transparent, and non-threatening sessions that examine these issues:

- *Did we meet the standard? If not, why not?*

- *What went right—and how can we sustain it?*

- *What went wrong—and what must we do to improve it?*

- *What must exactly be done to improve, and who must do it?*

- *How do we hold each other accountable to this higher standard?*

- *What lessons did we learn, and how do we use these lessons to shape our next mission?*

- *What impact do these lessons have on our processes, training, leader development, team structure, tools and equipment, and individual readiness?*

AARs must be conducted in an environment that fully embraces the process, without fear of incriminating statements or personal or professional repercussions. People who only care about the mission know that they cannot let their feelings get hurt when the light that we must shine on every element of the team's performance swings over to them. The discussions are not personal; there are no "thin skins."

An AAR is not a *love fest*. Sure, we can always spend time complementing each other and doling out credit, but in doing so we will *never* get to the heart of our issues. Sessions in which participants fail to call out anything that is less than perfect miss the mark. Without the willingness to be open to criticism and the passion to determine how to be the absolute best, AARs are a waste of time. We cannot allow the human inclination to want to *feel* good to outweigh the need to *be* great. As such, we cannot shy away from conflict; we must actively seek out those areas that need improvement.

One memorable evening at the NTC, I led an AAR covering a mission that we had completed that morning at 0700. (That's right, we finished by 0700. We started at 0200—2:00 a.m. for those of you who aren't versed in military time). It was a formal AAR conducted in one of the high-speed, fully instrumented trailers tucked up against the side of a mountain in the desert training area. The unit was a good one, having already deployed to Iraq and now in the cycle to return. Each of the participants had a patch on their right shoulder signifying combat experience, and each acted with the confidence that only comes from actual deployment.

In the back of the AAR trailer, out of sight of the participants, sat a four-star general, commander of all forces training for deployment to the Middle East. Needless to say, the pressure was on to have a good session. We spent two hours discussing what went well and what went not so well—and there was plenty of the latter. Emotions became strained at times as these tired warriors passionately debated where they needed to make improvements.

We filled whiteboards and notebooks with multiple entries on areas that needed to be fixed. We held each other accountable when members of the team didn't quite meet the standard. People called each other out when they thought they had let the team down by not giving their absolute best. While it was clear that the warriors of this unit had great love for one another, for those two hours at least, that affection was subordinated to their consuming passion to be a high-performing team.

The four-star VIP left the trailer before I could speak with him, causing me some concern that perhaps he didn't like what he had seen. Afterwards, though, my boss called me and passed along the general's feedback: "Tell Magness that was one of the best darned AARs I have ever attended. You know, I was worried about this unit's receptiveness to learning given that they had all recently returned from combat. But I could see the lights coming on and I know that the spirited debate was a sign of a well-led unit, committed to being the absolute best. Well done!"

The point was not that I led a good AAR, but that the session had served as a successful venue for learning. No one took offense at being called out—not even the unit commander. Everyone took ownership for their piece of the organization and acknowledged what had to be improved. They were not working together as a team, communication was poor, and they took far more (simulated) casualties on the objective than a seasoned unit like this should have. Despite the quantity of issues and shortcomings, this was an outstanding unit that would go on to serve with distinction in battle. The good ones have one goal: perfection. They never stop trying to get better. This was the same lesson I shared with my daughter after her setback in the school election, and is the basis of the AARs that we must make routine in the organizations, teams, schools, churches, and families we lead!

AAR Procedures

The first rule of AARs is . . . just do them! Any forum in which you can have honest discussions about improvement is a step in the right direction. We must create an environment that reflects a passionate commitment to learning and improvement without concern for turf or, as callous as it sounds, for personal feelings. Most importantly, we must believe that this is the means by which our organization can achieve greatness. *We* have to believe it first if we want our team to also value these disciplined settings, be committed to using them, and be ready to take action on what they learn.

AARs should focus almost exclusively on execution. They should examine critical leadership issues such as decision-making, communication, resource alignment, and how we established (or failed to establish) the situational awareness necessary for decisive action. They should comprehensively evaluate mission accomplishment and task completion through an assessment of performance objectives and key metrics and indices.

This is not to say that we don't want to look at our *planning* and *preparations*, but that we do so with an eye to their impact on execution. I always begin AARs with a brief discussion of what was *supposed* to happen during the mission, project, or event. Everyone must have a common understanding of what was expected to occur during execution. I allow the unit leader to describe his vision for the mission and proceed down the ranks to see if everyone understood those intentions. With a shared vision for the *plan*, we can check to see if our *preparations* were appropriately aligned (capable people, sufficient resources, and fully empowered and enabled teams). It is from this common framework that we can proceed to look at *what* happened and *why*.

I call it "peeling back the onion." AARs have to get to the *issues* that arose during execution. If necessary, we have to keep digging until the true source of problems is identified. In my experience, it is almost never the simple, surface problem that is inhibiting the team's performance. It is usually something deeper. Leaders must be prepared to continue to ask probing questions until we understand the real challenges identified by our teammates.

Once presented, discussions must focus on how to *fix* each problem, identifying responsibilities for *who* specifically will address these issues along with a *timeline* and the allocation of *resources* necessary to implement the solution. I will often begin a discussion by writing these headings (*issue, fix, who, timeline, resources*) on a board in column format, then filling in the blank spaces accordingly as we move through the AAR.

Leaders use leading question to get to the root causes of friction in execution. This also helps subordinates grow as they think through their problems and use their answers to come up with solutions they can own. Effective AARs include leading questions like:

- *What happened? Why did it happen?*

- ***Boss**: What specific guidance did you give for this project?*

- ***Team leaders**: Did you understand this guidance? How could we have made the boss' intent more clear to help you?*

- ***Team members**: When did you know the project was falling behind schedule? Who did you tell . . . and when?*

Leaders must be open to proposed fixes that come from any source. We have to cultivate the open dialogue that generates ideas from within the ranks. Top-down strategies and initiatives have a tendency to stifle innovation in those closest to the problem. The willingness to listen and engage every member of the team in AARs generates the sort of excitement and creativity that we want from people who will own their solutions.

"AARs are not critiques because they do not determine success or failure; rather, AARs are professional discussions of training events. Leaders and evaluators use AARs to tell a story about what was planned, what happened during the training, why it happened, and what could have been done differently to improve performance."

Army Field Manual 25-101

Get the "back row" involved in the AAR. Make sure everyone talks. Some of the greatest suggestions for improvement come from the trenches, so do not allow first-line leaders to dominate the discussion. I have found that the most effective AARs are the ones that encourage frank dialogue, allow the free flow of ideas from bottom to top, and create an environment where honest feedback and criticism are not only allowed, but are demanded.

Whoever leads the discussion must have an ear for solutions and have skills in facilitation. External resources, as I was during my time as an OC at the NTC, can leverage their understanding of industry-wide best practices. Most often, it is simply the responsibility of the leader to roll up his sleeves and take his team through this learning process.

Just to reinforce, here are the critical elements of a good AAR:

1. Focus on execution.

2. Peel back the onion.

3. Capture the *issue*, identify the *fix*, determine *who* is responsible, establish a *timeline*, and allocate *resources*.

4. Ask leading questions.

5. Listen for good ideas. Don't dominate the room.

6. Determine what *we* need to do to sustain our strengths and improve on our weaknesses. It's about the TEAM.

AAR Timing

Have you ever found yourself too busy "fighting your tail off" that you can't take a few minutes to save your tail from falling off? This is the challenge we all face. How do we stop the execution train long enough to do the maintenance necessary to keep the train rolling? How do we learn as part of routine operations and turn failure into future success?

Granted, the most difficult issue associated with AARs can be fitting them into an already full schedule. First and foremost, we must commit to doing them. They must be a routine part of the business process. Project delivery is not complete until the AAR is done. We don't hang up our hard hats for the day until we've executed our hot wash with the entire crew.

I am sure that the "gold standard" for this was developed at the NTC. Quite simply, we made sure that everyone understood that there was no higher priority for every one of the 3500+ soldiers and leaders at the completion of every single simulated battle or critical event. When it was time to learn, everything stopped and was subordinated to this top priority. The battle was literally put on pause for two hours so that people could devote their full attention to the AAR. From colonel to the brand new private, learning was the number one priority.

AARs should be conducted as close to the completion of each event as possible. For those items without such clear start and end points, AARs are held at the end of each project milestone or major activity. Some may consider conducting them every day—at the end of a shift or while closing up the store. For others, the end of a week may present an opportunity to review execution. AARs must be included on project schedules, event calendars, and milestone lists. Leaders have to lock them in, be rigorous, and accept no excuses. Some ideas include:

- Teachers can conduct AARs with their students at the end of each class to determine how effectively they presented the course content. They should be open to criticism and input that might improve student learning.

- Ministers can conduct AARs that include the feedback of their congregation and the church staff. AARs must review the previous week's religious programs and candidly assess whether they are meeting the needs of their ministry.

- Restaurant shift leaders can gather their team at the end of the night and solicit ideas on how to improve the dining experience for patrons.

- Sales teams can gather each week to measure their performance and identify product or process improvements that will lead to greater future sales.

In my experience, AARs usually take from 30 minutes to two hours. Anything more risks overwhelming most people's ability to absorb new learning. It also increases the likelihood of exceeding the typical human attention (and bladder retention) span! Leaders should work within this range, focus on a few things to improve, and strive for continuous, incremental gains. It is up to us to determine how and when to make AARs part of our standard operational procedures.

Granted, none of this is easy. There are always a thousand urgent issues that demand our attention. But the AAR simply has to become part of our standard procedures. It took the Army several years to institutionalize this approach to learning. Now it is part of the culture, part of every training event and combat mission, and a key component of the way they grow units and those who lead them. AARs are the cornerstone to growth and development. Nothing else is close.

Leader Business

Despite our focus on where we come up short and how we need to improve, we must take time to celebrate success! We have to reinforce positive behaviors and help people see what right looks like. I always start my AARs with awards, recognizing heroes with some small token of appreciation for their efforts. We cannot get so focused on trying to get better that we miss those occasions where we are already good!

Make sure everyone takes notes in AARs. This is not just a "check the block" activity. Teammates truly committed to learning are passionate about improvement. Key points must be written down and commitments must be captured to ensure accountability.

Once written down, go the next step and find a way to share these lessons with others—inside and outside the organization. Put them in an email, in the company newsletter, or on the unit intranet or bulletin board. Invest in the mechanics for a more structured process that archives lessons and makes them available for future reference (searchable, sortable, etc.). Connect the dots and write a professional article that helps others benefit from our lessons.

Think others can't benefit from our learning? On April 26, 2003 a Marine Corps first sergeant, during the initial invasion of Iraq, took the time to enter his unit's lessons into an email. This action began the distribution of key warfighting lessons that circled the globe and were shared with combat units worldwide, to include trainers like me at the NTC. His comments on things like individual equipment, battle drills, and complex urban operations immediately began to shape the way my own team prepared for future battles. Thankfully, this warrior took the time to write down his lessons and share them with others.

The best AARs I facilitated were the ones in which I did the least talking. Good unit leaders would take over and set the conditions for learning. They accepted criticism readily and held themselves accountable. I could often simply frame the discussion, and then let them talk it out while I captured the issues and their suggested solutions. I could close out the topic with some suggested best practices and then move on to the next issue. Good units, and their leaders, have a sincere desire to learn and to grow. It is truly a beautiful thing to behold!

Whether on the battlefield, in middle school elections, on Wall Street, or on Main Street, leaders must take the time to learn through AARs. Adding them as a routine part of operations will help our teams avoid repeating past mistakes, achieve future success, and maintain plenty of distance between us and our competitors.

Marching Orders

* *How can you make AARs a routine part of your operations?*

* *Do you have a culture in which you can be comfortable with*

lower-ranking people pointing out your shortcomings? Is there a forum to do so?

- *Do your "hot-washes" or post-mission reviews get to the heart of the issue or just touch the surface of challenges on your team?*

Chapter 16

Train to Win

"There are no secrets to success. It is the result of preparation,
hard work, and learning from failure."
GENERAL COLIN L. POWELL

I have been fortunate. I cannot begin to count up the investment that my organization has made in me to set me up for success. Four years at West Point gave me the basic understanding of leadership that I would need to stand in front of a 30-man platoon. Airborne and Ranger training taught me the fundamentals of small unit leadership, about overcoming adversity, and teamwork. The National Training Center gave me an understanding of the business of leaders (good enough plans, building teams and aligning resources, mission accomplishment, and learning through AARs). I have been training for 30 years.

I believe I represent the answer to the question of whether leaders are born or made. In high school, I was a selfish, awkward teen with not a strand of leadership DNA in my very skinny frame. Now 30 years later, I'm still learning, still growing, and still building leadership muscle density. I am thankful that those who assessed me at 18 didn't give up on me or write me off because I wasn't "born" to lead. Perhaps they recognized that with training (and a LOT of it), I could realize my potential. It was a lesson not lost on me. I am a definite believer in the power of training and the obligation to provide training to the teams we lead.

Training impacts each of the primary responsibilities of a leader. You remember what they are, right?

1. **Accomplish the mission.** Training produces capable, competent warriors and leaders, ready to tackle any challenge.

2. **Take care of people.** Nothing says "I care" like making an investment in the growth and development of others.

3. **Efficient use of resources.** There may be no more important element in the budget than what we allocate toward training our team.

We Train . . . Because We Care

Field Marshal Rommel found "first class training" to be the best form of soldier welfare. When it came to taking care of his subordinates, he ranked it higher than pay and benefits, time off, recognition, or any other traditional component of troop morale. Nothing demonstrated a greater concern for subordinates, he reasoned, than providing the individual and collective skills that would enable mission success or, in their case, victory in battle.

You will find this same philosophy shared by U.S. Army leaders today. Tough, mission-focused, realistic training enables soldiers and units to do their jobs. It keeps them alive to fight again. It gives them confidence in themselves and in each other. It provides the repetitions on key leadership tasks that create the muscle density we expect from our battle-tested warriors. Like Rommel, our military leaders know it does no good to coddle people to gain short term gratification, only to leave them ill-prepared when it really matters.

Nowhere in the military is training more central to an organization's mission than my favorite place, the National *Training* Center. Long recognized as the premier practice battlefield for combat units, the NTC regularly affirms the following military training principles:

1. Focus your training.

2. Leave no one behind.

3. Develop your leaders.

4. Every failure is an opportunity to learn.

It is important to note that the NTC is the battleground for *training*, not *testing*. Soldiers develop themselves in conditions that provide the freedom to try new techniques and to experiment with innovative approaches to problem solving. Leaders are encouraged to take measured risks and make decisions. People are measured not by failure, but on how high they reach and whether they learn. If it is true that "pain leads to gain," then it is certainly true that there is some real growing going on at the NTC!

Some define luck as the intersection of opportunity and preparation. Fortune inevitably comes to those who train. This is how we prepare our bodies for the hard work of execution. This is how we prepare our minds for the strain of leading others and the heavy responsibilities that come from being out in front. Training prepares leaders—and those they lead—to be ready for the opportunities that will come. It is in so doing, I believe, that we *create* our own luck.

Let us therefore not limit this kind of intense learning experience to our combat troops. We owe it to all of our teammates to ensure that they are ready to do battle. CEOs need practice on public speaking and communicating a shared vision. Middle managers need to be drilled on decision making and providing feedback to their team. Teachers need instruction on new educational materials. First responders must rehearse their drills for any number of emergency scenarios. Retail clerks should practice dealing with customer issues. Chefs need to practice preparing different meals before offering customers a new menu. Success is never an accident. *Everyone* needs to train to win.

Focus Your Training

Because we all have limits to what we are able to apply toward our education requirements, we had better be smart about how and what we train. Expenditures must be focused on essential tasks, beginning with the most critical and working down until we run out of time or money. Leaders must be involved in prioritizing the tasks and drills that must be rehearsed, along with the collective skills that we need from our teams. We have to be able to align what we do in training with the deliverables we need to be successful. In any setting, we can have high confidence that we will get the behaviors we train and the positive performance that we re-inforce through focused training.

> *"Most people never run far enough on their first wind to find out they've got a second. Give your dreams all you've got and you'll be amazed at the energy that comes out of you."*
>
> **William James**

Leaders place top priority on training outlays that enable mission accomplishment while making the call on those that, while nice to have, will not return on their investment. They assess current and future skill needs and seek creative ways to develop capabilities in things like crisis management and decision making; customer service skills; the integration and use of new technologies; communication in all of its various forms; and, of course, my favorite: leadership. These are all likely to be the sort of tasks with direct relationship to job #1: *execution*.

Military leaders usually conduct a formal analysis to identify training priorities for their team. Doing so yields the focused training requirements for individuals, leaders, and teams that contribute directly to mission accomplishment. Our training needs are simply outputs from the detailed mission analysis we perform in developing our plans. Tasks must be broken down all the way to individual team member skills. Essential tasks *must* be trained. Each employee must be assessed against the list of tasks they must perform. Those things that can already be done to standard can be crossed off the list, allowing us to move on to other requirements. This disciplined approach to analyzing the mission, determining priorities, and assessing talent, gives focus to our training investments.

I briefly mentioned in the last chapter the need for every member of the team to have an Individual Development Plan (IDP). This document should track the development path for each of our employees. It should be reviewed during performance counseling so that everyone understands what they need to do to meet mission requirements, how they will grow within the organization, and when they can expect to be trained. This system is informative not just to the employee, but also to the supervisor, providing the ability to forecast and align training resources.

After four years of observing training at the NTC, I am confident that focused training has a high return on investment (ROI) and serious potential for both individual and unit improvement. The greatest gains are realized when we follow these *Leader Business* principles:

- **Crawl before you walk, walk before you run.** We must ensure we address the "troop level" skills before we start thinking about complex tasks or activities. Increase the degree of difficulty with each training repetition or for more seasoned teams.

- **Train by doing, not by watching.** Improvement is maximized through participative learning. Minimize classroom "death by PowerPoint" sessions and take maximum advantage of "hands on" training opportunities.

- **Make practice harder than the real thing.** Don't hold back during training sessions. Failure *is* an option . . . during training. Push subordinates to the point of failure, conduct good AARs, and watch growth and development explode. Astronauts and fighter pilots often talk about the rigors of the simulator being, in many ways, more challenging than actual flight. This was exactly the sentiment we sought in our training at the NTC. We wanted our units to write us to say that the challenges they faced in training made much of what they did in combat anti-climatic. I am proud to say that my team received a lot of feedback along these lines.

Leave No One Behind

Recall our discussion on empowerment and the importance of building teams with members who truly have the freedom to be creative, take risks, and solve problems? Remember the critical elements of empowerment: education, opportunity, and feedback? This should be the focus of our entire training and development program, and why it is so important that leaders recognize it as a primary responsibility. Education comes from training; opportunity is the result of training and developmental assignments and tasks; and feedback is what we provide our teammates as part of both.

In my experience, the number one contributor to positive morale is when people know that their contribution matters. We need every single member of the team to truly embrace this concept. No one can be left behind. They *know* they are valued when they see the investments—in the form of education, opportunity, and feedback—made to help them grow and develop. When people get all three, there is nothing they won't do for the team or for their leader.

Two key groups that I would encourage any leader to pay attention to are new employees and future leaders. The former must be made to feel like they are part of something meaningful from the very beginning. They need the skills and tools to do their job, as well as the orientation and training that gives them the competence and the confidence to do it well. The latter is truly the legacy for any leader: the steps we take to prepare the next generation of leaders. Just as a chain is only as strong as its weakest link, a lack of training will quickly manifest itself in the neglected area (poor customer feedback, reduced sales, etc.), especially with new employees and new supervisors.

In 2009, I led the orientation program for incoming District Commanders (newly designated CEOs) for the Army Corps of Engineers, people who fit both categories of emerging leaders *and* new employees for this public engineering organization. What a great thing it was to be a part of a group of seasoned commanders training the "new guys," peers helping peers prepare for the first 90 days of command. I was thrilled to see the Chief of Engineers, the lieutenant general who headed the entire 35,000-person agency, spend almost the entire week with us. He recognized how important it was to personally make his priorities known, and that these new leaders (two levels below him in the chain of command) received his vision, strategy, and critical missions directly from him. We would all do well to be a part of our new employee and emerging leader training programs to that extent!

While every member of the team needs personal and professional development, I am not suggesting everyone gets everything they want in this area. These can be difficult calls for leaders to make. It's our job to manage resources while ensuring that no one is left behind. The prioritization and distribution of training opportunities, and the creative ways by which we can improve everyone, are the result of focusing our training within a culture that values every member of the team.

When resources are a constraint, we have to seek out alternative ways of providing education and training. Classroom instruction and other traditional programs may not be the most efficient means of delivery for key skills. Sometimes, we don't need high levels of investment. Leaders simply must be creative and leverage the full arsenal of available training tools, including: on-line courses, developmental assignments and mentorship programs, brown bag lunch seminars, sabbaticals, 360-degree feedback, night and weekend continuing education programs, and any form of training that pushes subordinates to failure . . . and subsequent growth. Again, we want our practice to be harder than the real thing. It often takes little more than imagination to do so.

Develop Your Leaders

We get capable subordinates in direct proportion to what we do to train them. Most people are not born with an understanding of the fundamentals of the business of leaders. They need training on how to plan, prepare, and execute the mission, as well as how to lead growth-inducing AARs. They need to be mentored on the skills required for their current job and, more important, for their next position.

Remember when we talked about how important it is to hire well and get the right person on-board to meet the needs of the team? It is just as important that we retain those we already have. This means we have to train the ones we've got to become better leaders. We have to grow capable subordinates who understand the business, who are competent in decision-making, and who have sufficient tools to develop within the organization. Similarly, we must develop our emerging leaders, knowing that these internal hires will ultimately fill the majority of our leadership ranks. All of this requires that we balance our training investments: current versus future needs, technical versus leadership skills, current versus prospective leaders, and training versus mission execution.

Training in leader development never stops. I have received formal instruction on technical skills and leadership fundamentals at every rank, again usually focused on what I would need to know in my *next* assignment. It doesn't even stop when Army leaders become generals. Newly promoted brigadier (one-star) generals go to a six-week "capstone" course to prepare them for service at their new grade. They get direct feedback from senior generals and retired "gray beards" in training exercises at least every 18 months. Even with 25-35 years of service, our generals are still learning.

You've likely heard the vignette about the two woodsmen in a competition to chop down the most trees. One went at it furiously, never taking a break, giving everything he had without a pause. The other pulled away for 10 minutes every hour or so to whet his stone and sharpen his blade. It was the second man who far outpaced the first in leveling the forest. I have found that it is no different in leader

> *"All of the top achievers I know are life-long learners . . . looking for new skills, insights, and ideas. If they're not learning, they're not growing . . . not moving toward excellence."*
>
> **Denis Waitley**

development. We have to pull back periodically and sharpen our respective leadership blades. At all levels, people need time to think about their profession, connect the dots, and generate new ideas. Leadership is a series of sprints, interspersed with well-timed moments to catch our breath, sharpen the axe, and prepare for the next race.

In fact, brain research on how we learn has proved this very point. Our brains need time to digest and reflect on new learning in order to effectively incorporate it into our mental frameworks. This is the great shortfall of traditional teaching/training models that rely on lecture and "death by Powerpoint"—too much information delivered too fast for the brain to process. Without that time, we tend to lose a lot of new information, dots are not connected, and our blades get dull.

AAR Everything

Leaders who treat every event as a learning opportunity know the importance of stopping, assessing performance, and conducting AARs. Did you miss a quarterly performance metric? Why—and how can you do better? Did you achieve your team goals? What can be improved—and how do you sustain what went well?

Just as with traditional training and education forums, quality AARs focus principally on things that lead to higher productivity and enhanced results. Every failure is an opportunity for improvement and organizational growth. Every success is an occasion to identify areas for incremental improvement. A disciplined, rigorous, no-holds-barred examination of what happened, why it happened, and how to sustain or improve team actions is essential to achieve, or sustain, excellence. AARs make every experience a learning opportunity in at least these three ways:

1. **AARs** *supplement* **the training menu.** Even when budgets are tight or opportunities to go outside for training are sparse, there is always time for a debrief. Using the techniques we covered in the last chapter, we can use these sessions to learn from each other and to stimulate new ways to solve problems.

2. **AARs** *complete* **the training experience.** We are not done with our training until we have reviewed what we have learned. Similarly, we have not completed the session until we have given feedback to the instructor, helping both the teacher and the students think about better ways to train.

3. **AARs** *produce* **more capable trainers.** The professional dialogue that occurs among warriors, unconcerned with rank or their own feelings, will usually fill up entire notebooks of things to work on. These become the tasks that must be addressed in future training opportunities. Nothing exposes the "holes in our swing" like tough, standards-based training—and the AARs that follow.

Leader Business

In the military, training a unit and equipping soldiers and their leaders for success is a primary leadership responsibility. It must therefore be one of the major criteria against which we measure subordinate leader performance, namely how well are they accomplishing their training mission? Are they improving their people and their teams? Are they using all of their training resources? Like Rommel, are they ensuring the skills necessary for mission accomplishment through first class training?

Despite the formal designation of "training officers" in military units, it is the commander, the unit leader, who is ultimately held accountable for this critical task. It is no different in any other leadership role. Supervisors, not the HR staff, are uniquely responsible for training their team. Leaders must participate in formal reviews of training needs, prioritize requirements, allocate training resources, design training exercises, and lead AARs. It is *not* someone else's job.

Leaders can never settle for the excuse that they are too busy to train. We will end up using that crutch until we wake up one day and find ourselves, or the teams we lead, irrelevant. People will always require development. The future will always demand new skills to maintain competitiveness in our respective markets. We can never allow ourselves to become *that* busy.

Consider that even while deployed to war zones such as Iraq and Afghanistan, military commanders still embrace the critical role of training the force. They do so by balancing immediate mission requirements with recurring training tasks such as weapons qualification, military education, small unit drills, and the ever-present AARs. Training is not a distraction from the mission. Even during wartime, it is *the* principal enabler of mission accomplishment. In a war where the enemy changes constantly, training is not just a good idea—it has life and death consequences.

As leaders, we have to invest in continuously improving ourselves. We are all works in progress and are, by no means, fully developed. We should all be looking at how we can improve on our weaknesses, how we can better leverage our strengths, and how we can be exposed to new learning and the sort of ideas that will stimulate our deepest leadership muscle fibers. We have to be comfortable taking ourselves off-line to think, to rest, and to sharpen our respective axes.

These days, it is critical that we all take a portion of our training resources and allocate it toward character, values, and ethics training. If there are any doubts about the need for this type of skill development, pick up any recent newspaper. The business battlefield is littered with the remains of once-powerful organizations and leaders who assessed incorrectly the character training needs within their respective teams or themselves. We need to ensure that our subordinates have a fundamental understanding of ethics, workplace regulations, financial stewardship, and other hot character issues. Trust me, this is not political correctness. Sustained success is only possible with teammates who trust each other and share the same values.

West Point cadets embody the very character that we all seek in our organizations. It's no accident. These students complete hundreds of hours of ethics training. Formal leadership, philosophy, and behavioral science classes are a major part of their core curriculum. They are "grown"—from the ground up—with regard to character development. Leadership opportunities from day one of the "plebe" year further serve as training for their personal and professional character. Nothing is taken for granted.

Finally, it is worth the reminder that we get the teams that we prepare. If we don't train, we cannot expect to have much promise for the future. New opportunities will present themselves and we will not be ready. Our people will not be legitimately empowered for the demands we will place on them. Employees who value growth and development will go somewhere else to find it. Even in times of difficult budgets, we cannot eliminate training. We have to continue to build and sustain the team to meet both current and future mission requirements.

If we are not investing in training, rest assured that our competition most certainly is. When we fail to balance current and future skill requirements, we miss those narrow windows of opportunity. If we are not constantly analyzing the mission essential training requirements, to include character development, of every single member of our team, one of them will become our chain's weakest link. And if we are not training ourselves and sharpening our respective blades, we will soon not be qualified to lead our own teams. No easy tasks, especially with all the other things we are supposed to be doing, but that's why they need us!

Marching Orders

- *What portion of your budget do you allocate to training? How do you hold people accountable to do it?*

- *Are you conducting the sort of deliberate analysis necessary to identify the training needs of your team?*

- *What are you doing to structure your new employee orientation and leader development programs to meet your intentions?*

Chapter 17
The Leader-Coach

*"Better than a thousand days of diligent study
is one day with a great teacher."*
JAPANESE PROVERB

Y ou have likely heard the quote from H.L. Mencken that says, "Those who can, do; those who can't, teach." Seems a bit cynical, doesn't it? Do we really want the ranks of our teachers, coaches, and consultants to be filled with people who are not capable of doing the job themselves? Yet more and more, it seems this quote is becoming fulfilled in the modern day translation, "Those who can, do; those who can't (or won't, or think somehow that the 'doing' is beneath them), become our leaders." Don't bother them with the details. They are the "big picture types." If an employee needs coaching, mentoring, or teaching, their plan is invariably to contract some outside help.

Too many leaders that I know fall into the trap, as they move up the ranks, of thinking that leadership is solely "big picture" visionary stuff. They don't want to be bothered with "the doing," since they think their job is to climb up the mast and see over the horizon. You show me someone who believes this, and I will show you a leader who doesn't understand what is really happening within his formation. These are the leaders who sound convincing at the shareholder meetings, yet have no clue about the underpinnings of the company. We cannot fall into this trap. If the visionary stuff was all that leaders needed to worry about, I could have stopped writing after Chapter One! But by now, you and I both know there is so much more to being an effective leader.

My experience in working with hundreds of leaders is that it is easy to fire off orders to others, but much more difficult to assess whether they truly understand what we are asking of them. Too many leaders seem resistant to getting into the trenches and teaching people *how* to do *what* we want from them. We elevate ourselves, beat our chest, and say that we are leaders, not managers, and that we cannot be bothered with details. This all-too-familiar scenario is so dangerous, yet is prevalent in many organizations today.

Let's make the case now for the leader-coach. Let's finish up this discussion of the leader's responsibilities by looking at how we facilitate learning by coaching, jumping into the arena and passing along our wisdom, helping people solve problems, not just assigning them. In other words: *Those who can, do; those who lead, coach.*

Learning From Coaches

By now, you are familiar with my experiences at the Army's National Training Center (NTC), where I served for four years as a coach for training unit leaders preparing for deployment. Every supervisor, from brand new lieutenant to the most senior colonel, had a dedicated mentor like me who served to provide feedback, capture and share lessons learned and best practices, and to inspire and challenge his counterpart to increasingly higher levels of excellence. This was the key strength of the NTC learning experience. It was like weightlifting with an experienced spotter to help with proper form and to push for increasingly higher weights. Only this time, it was the leadership muscles that we were targeting.

Successful leaders in all facets of life demonstrate a commitment to learning and continuous improvement. But as we discussed in the last chapter, education in a formal classroom setting is only part of professional growth. Effective leaders know they cannot *hope* for improvement, and that they will not achieve greatness alone. They need the tough love and engagement that comes from one-on-one contact with others. Just as we provided each leader at the NTC with a coach, so anyone committed to continuous growth and development needs coaching.

Do you want to improve as a leader? Get a coach. Hire an outside consultant or find a mentor who can serve as your leadership "spotter" and help you add leadership muscle density. Are you ready to make your team a legitimate learning organization? Establish a coaching and mentoring network and make the necessary investments so that your subordinates may similarly reap the benefits of dedicated trainers and teachers.

Here's the point: If we want to be truly great leaders, if we want to transform our teams into learning organizations, then we must climb down from the mast and fulfill our role as leader-coach. This task is too important to be left solely to outsiders or human resource professionals. This is what leaders do. That makes it, like so many of the other responsibilities we have discussed thus far, *Leader Business*.

The Case for Coaching

Recent labor force trends have reinforced the leader's obligation to develop subordinates. The mantra for today's workers is often, "Develop me or I'm out of here!" Today's workforce craves the type of positive, inspiring engagement from their leaders that enables personal and professional growth. They yearn for new skills. They want to see the big picture.

Yet a recent Gallup poll found that only 17% of employees report any kind of investment in their relationship from their manager in the previous three months. Equally disconcerting is the statistic that fewer than 1 in 5 workers consider their boss to be a close friend. This comes despite the finding that employees who have a close friendship with their manager are 2.5 times as likely to be satisfied with their jobs. No doubt this satisfaction translates into high morale, improved retention rates, and most importantly, better employee and team performance. The bottom line: leaders who personally invest in their relationship with employees impact . . . well, the bottom line.

This is not to suggest that leaders should be "buddy-buddy" with their teammates. There is a necessary separation between the manager and the employee. It is possible, however, to invest in personal relationships with those whom we lead—to be friends even if we are the boss. People thrive on one-on-one interaction, especially from their supervisor. They need to hear that what they do makes a difference. Nothing reinforces people's belief in what they are doing, and that they are doing it with the full trust and confidence of their superiors, like the sort of feedback, teaching, and coaching that people get from personal relationships with their boss. Personal coaching matters *that* much.

> "The boss drives people; the leader coaches them. The boss depends on authority; the leader on good will. The boss inspires fear; the leader inspires enthusiasm. The boss says 'I'; the leader says 'we.' The boss fixes the blame for the breakdown; the leader fixes the breakdown. The boss says, 'go!'; the leader says, 'Let's go!'"
>
> **H. Gordon Selfridge**

Coaching at all levels serves to bridge the connectivity gap while providing a mechanism for growth in learning organizations. Leader-coaches help people achieve their best performance. They push subordinates to new levels of excellence, inspire them to believe in themselves, and invest in the personal and professional development of each team member.

Successful leader-coaches are the ones down on the factory floor, in the classrooms, or walking the halls listening to employee issues, helping them work through difficult problems. They engage emerging leaders on issues of character, vision, and career progression. They serve as sounding boards for new ideas. They coach, teach, and mentor subordinates on the tactics and techniques of effective leaders.

Experienced leaders recognize that there is clearly a time and place for top-down, directive leadership. But the more frequent, more rewarding leadership style is much more personal, with the leader as coach. This approach meets the needs of subordinates who desire engagement and development and provides a positive forum for learning within an organization. In effect, leader-coaches teach teammates "how to fish," instead of merely giving them fish or, worse yet, telling them to "go fish" without investing in the skills and tools necessary to make them good fishermen!

Coaching Fundamentals

In his book, *My American Journey*, Colin Powell tells a story of losing his weapon while on maneuvers in Germany as a young Army lieutenant. Now for those who don't know, this is a big deal with potentially devastating implications. Lieutenant Powell's commander instead used that event as an opportunity for growth. Captain Miller successfully made his point on the criticality of such a mistake without destroying the confidence of the man who would later become Chairman of the Joint Chiefs of Staff and Secretary of State.

Colin Powell rightly points out that we'd likely dismiss a military leader for such a mistake today. Captain Miller held Lieutenant Powell accountable, yet did so in a professionally developing way. Now *that* is good coaching! Whether coaching subordinates or soliciting the mentorship of someone in your own journey, consider these basic principles for leadership coaching:

1. **Coaches provide candid feedback.** One-on-one coaching is the opportunity to tell it like it is. Leaders who invest in this sort of relationship understand that there is at least one person who will give it straight, focusing on areas for growth. Any formal coaching or mentoring relationship must begin with a clear understanding, from both parties, that the "rules of engagement" include the requirement for frank, honest dialogue.

   It does no good to simply tear people down. They will go somewhere else for their mentorship. Worse yet, in that climate, learning simply stops. People shut down. On the contrary, it is possible to provide feedback in a positive, encouraging manner. Leaders invest the time to build people up, providing feedback and suggesting positive means to improve. The focus shifts away from the behavior and toward the means to correct it. People thrive on this sort of engagement with their leaders.

2. **Good coaching is about self-discovery.** Leading questions help identify motives (*Why did you make the decision you did?*) and alternatives (*What else might you have done in that situation?*). A good coach helps teammates solve their own problems. Most self-aware people know their shortcomings. Usually, we won't need to point out their problems. We need to help them think through what they can do to correct them. Again, this approach is always positive and keeps teammates hungry for this sort of engagement with their leaders.

3. **A good coach holds subordinates accountable without beating them down.** One way is to establish standards and expectations—together. The fear of disappointing not only their coach but themselves is usually enough to ensure standards are met. Goals and objectives must be measurable and reviewed regularly. Failures should be viewed as opportunities for growth while successes celebrated, yet similarly reviewed for lessons learned. Good coaches are fair but firm, always pushing to new levels of excellence and ensuring that mutually established conditions and standards are met.

4. **Leader-coaches learn how to lead AARs.** As we have highlighted in this section on learning, every event, milestone, completed mission, project success or failure is an opportunity for positive, inspiring coaching. Effective leader-coaches know they must be ready to stop what they are

doing, rally the troops, and review performance. Coaches serve as facilitators for these sessions. This is the sort of forum in which we can highlight opportunities for growth, share best practices, and update team processes, procedures, and systems.

5. **Coaching reinforces the types of behaviors we have highlighted here as *Leader Business*.** We can use discussions as opportunities to help people understand where they fit in the shared vision, to give feedback on good enough plans, big ideas, and new initiatives, and to reward the performance that we seek to reinforce (measured risk-taking, effective decision making, and bold, aggressive action).

Coach to Win

People who embrace this powerful role of leader-coach reap not only the benefits of improved individuals, but quickly realize the exponential improvement in the entire organization. Teams recognize that their leader is engaged, competent, and truly invested in learning. People want to succeed, if for no other reason than for the positive feedback from their teammates and their coach.

Engagement with a leader-coach improves morale and enhances team motivation and collective job satisfaction. Subordinates who know that their leaders are invested in their development will hold themselves accountable to the team and mission accomplishment. Employees thrive in an environment in which they are confident that their contribution matters.

Investments by the leader-coach serve to broaden organizational situational awareness. It is through coaching that we can help employees understand the bigger picture and the contribution of each individual to the team. We can help them see themselves (both strengths and weaknesses), see the enemy (threats or lessons learned from competitors) and see the terrain (operational conditions and the road ahead).

Few leaders have invested in future leaders as deliberately as former General Electric CEO Jack Welch. His off-site leadership sessions were legendary . . . and mandatory. He used them to train and grow his leadership team, personally instilling in them a sense of purpose, vision, and accountability. He knew intimately both the strengths and weaknesses of emerging leaders, as well as their potential for higher levels of responsibility, because he was disciplined about dedicating his time and energy toward their growth.

> *"The mediocre teacher tells. The good teacher explains. The superior teacher demonstrates. The great teacher inspires."*
>
> **William A. Ward**

As was the case at GE, both formal and informal coach/mentor programs enable the identification of future leaders. Time spent together in a coaching relationship exposes each participant to new ideas, provides time for probing questions, and serves as a valuable assessment tool on the future leaders of the organization. Those who invest in coaching generally have the most effective succession programs. As coaches, we are personally and uniquely responsible for the development of our future leaders.

Leader Business

Leader-coaches invest in subordinates, not just one, but two levels below their own. Time spent with those second tier leaders helps inculcate the desired culture of learning at the level where it can really stick. These middle managers and emerging leaders are not only the future of the organization, but they thrive in an environment with unfiltered access to the vision, goals, and professional instruction of their boss.

Those who recognize this critical responsibility of the leader know that there is a right way and a wrong way to develop others through coaching. For every chair-throwing, player-berating, out-of-control coach, there is someone like Duke basketball's Mike Krzyzewski, 2010 NCAA National Championship coach . . . and, as I mentioned previously (and quite proudly), West Point class of 1969. Listen to "Coach K's" approach to developing others: "*People have to be given the freedom to show the heart they possess. I think it's a leader's responsibility to provide that type of freedom. And I believe it can be done through relationships and family. Because if a team is a real family, its members want to show you their hearts.*"

It most certainly is possible to engage with people at the emotional level, to believe in and empower our teammates, and provide them the form of leadership that produces championships year after year. Coach K says, "I don't look at myself as a basketball coach. I look at myself as a leader who happens to coach basketball."

So I'm not suggesting that we all become business coaches, but rather that we fulfill our obligations as leaders who also happen to coach those with whom we serve in our businesses. Here are a few of the techniques that enable successful coaching on any court:

- **Listen first.** Good coaches understand that they must seek first to understand others before they try to communicate their own message. Coaching begins with listening—to the dreams, aspirations, and personal and professional goals of the employee. There are no "cookie-cutter" solutions to most leadership challenges. Instead, leader-coaches listen before speaking and learn before teaching. We cannot solve everyone's problems. Let them work through it, ask leading questions, and guide them to their own solutions.

- **Inspire greatness.** There is no ceiling for a team led by a positive, inspiring leader-coach. Effective coaches demonstrate in word and deed a passionate pursuit of excellence, motivating others to join them in their journey. No one likes a cynic. No one will follow a depressed, uninspiring, passionless leader into battle. Don't be *that* person. Instead, create a positive view of the future and use every interaction to help people see their role in reaching those increasingly higher levels of excellence. Help people believe in themselves and give them the confidence to be the best. Yeah . . . be *that* leader!

- **Create a sense of TEAM.** Coach people in a way that helps them understand their role, the goals, objectives, and shared vision of the organization, and gives them confidence not just in their own abilities, but in the conviction of their coach. People need to know that we are in this thing with them, that we have no motivation other than the growth and development of every member of the team and the learning that enables excellence. Effective coaches use "we" (*How can we be better?*) instead of "you" (*What are you doing wrong?*) to demonstrate the concept of team and a shared commitment to success.

- **Encourage risk taking.** Leader-coaches seek out opportunities to reward those teammates who willingly take on the difficult projects and big challenges. They pick people up off the ground and help them learn from their failures without dampening their aggressiveness. They teach them things like risk assessment and mitigation, and continue to push them to pursue bold, audacious goals.

- **Share best practices.** Leader-coaches pass along lessons learned from across the team and enable the learning of everyone. Successful coaches are the ones who are looking across the industry for new techniques and emerging technologies to spiral into the organization. They pass along the wisdom that comes from experience, sharing successes and failures (including their own) for the benefit of those they coach.

Let me end this section on learning with a story that shows the power of passionate leadership and the role of the leader-coach. One of my brothers came across this letter, sent to the wife of a Vietnam-era military officer from one of his former subordinates:

> *Although it has been 35 years since I last saw your husband, he made a deep, lasting, and profound impression in my life. I served with (him) at the 2/32 Artillery at Tay Ninh. I was a captain, one of your husband's Assistant S3s.*
>
> *You see, your husband was more than just a boss to me. I was a young captain, trying to find my way in Vietnam, in the Army, and in life as well. (Your husband) was always there as a guide, a coach, in many ways a bit of a father and big brother wrapped into one. He was someone who was always there with leadership and wisdom, not the cold military dictates that were so common in those days.*
>
> *It has been said that we are all the sum of the people we choose to allow to influence our lives. My life has been made much better by your husband's tutelage. Your husband was a good man. I'm sure you miss him so very much, and I just wanted to thank you and his family, in any way I could, for the positive impact your husband had in my life.*

You can see clearly how the impact of a leader-coach goes well beyond the normal senior-subordinate relationship. Coaching does matter. There are great coaches available to us. Seek out a positive, inspiring, ethical leader and solicit their advice. Our leadership can always use the stretching that comes from the interaction with others—whether they are a superior one or two levels above us, a mentor, or an executive coach. The accountability and growth potential, no matter the source, is well worth the investment.

But if we want to really see our leadership take off, we need to become leader-coaches. In so doing, we will quickly realize that coaching is a two-way street. Investing in the growth and learning of others yields a high return on investment . . . in our own leadership ability and in the effectiveness of the organizations we lead. It's a win/win.

No sports team can be successful without the positive, inspiring leadership of its coach. It is no different in the military—or in business. Evidenced by the young officer learning life lessons in Vietnam from my Dad, then-Major Tom Magness, there is a desperate need for inspirational, compassionate engagement from a leader-coach. Our employees, teammates, and fellow warriors are waiting for us to fill this role. We can't let them down!

Marching Orders

*   *Who is your coach? Who can you work with to grow your own leadership?*

*   *Are you comfortable getting down in the trenches and showing people what they need to do to be successful?*

*   *What are you doing to enable the success of your teammates one and two levels below your own? Are you accessible to them?*

Conclusion
Take Charge of Your Unit

"When placed in command—take charge."
GENERAL H. NORMAN SCHWARZKOPF

The purpose of this book was to describe the all-encompassing duties and responsibilities of a leader and what we might do to take charge in any situation. The time is now for immediate action. Whether we are given a new assignment, ready to energize our old job, or simply seated at the head of the table and asked to be the "decider," the business of leaders is to be up to the task. Let's be calm and use our leadership muscles as we sort through the facts, analyze alternatives, make decisions, and stay focused on the mission. Let's take charge through our involvement in every facet of planning, preparation, execution, and learning.

In 25 years of leading others, I have found that there are three types of people in leadership positions: those who make things happen, those who let things happen, and those who wonder *what* happened. Let's *make* things happen! When in charge, let's take charge. Recall, friends, that leadership is about *action*. Leadership is a verb. Taking charge, applying the elements of this book to any position or situation, is what leaders *do*!

I have taken command of six units: my first job as platoon leader at Fort Hood, Texas; company command in Nuremberg, Germany; Army Corps of Engineers district command in Detroit, Los Angeles, and Kabul, Afghanistan; and the leadership of my training team—the Sidewinders—at the National Training Center. The very act of taking over a new position, no matter how many times I have done so, is a humbling, sweaty-palms experience.

In the Army, we assume new leadership positions through a formal ceremony: the change of command. The troops line up neatly on the parade field, each unit led by its respective commander. Beside each commander is the flag bearer, proudly carrying the unit's colors that signify its official designation and role within the command.

The ceremony is completed when the higher headquarters commander takes the colors, officially relinquishing the outgoing leader of his responsibilities, and passes them to the incoming commander. This military tradition brings formal closure to the tenure of the old leader and signals the transfer of the burdens of command to the new one. The new commander has full authority and the immediate loyalty and obedience of his unit.

What I have learned is that the change of command ceremony is only the beginning. What follows is the hard part—to earn the trust and confidence of my team, to step out and be a leader, to take command of my troops and lead them into battle. The *action* part of being the leader is just beginning, in which each of the elements of this book plays out every day, in everything we do.

Some of us, when we honestly assess it, will discover that while we may already be in a leadership position, we have never really *taken charge*. We may not have fully embraced all of the responsibilities described here as *Leader Business*. Perhaps we need a leadership "do over." Further delay only amplifies the failure to have gotten it right the first time. There is no time like the present to take command of our respective teams, and start acting like a leader.

Before Taking Charge

Rushing head first into any leadership role without having done your homework is a recipe for embarrassment and mission failure. Understand the environment in which you will operate. Look internally and examine the functions of the current organization. Assess existing strengths and weaknesses. Look externally to understand current and future trends and organizational opportunities and threats. Understand the financial underpinnings of the company. Know where you fit in the larger corporate picture. In other words, keep up with the running estimate of your organizational and personal SWOT. Update it continuously.

Take time to think. Capture your initial findings and arrange a list of questions you might wish to explore upon accepting the new challenge. Prepare an initial set of goals and objectives based on your research and understanding of the operational environment.

> *"Visualize this thing you want. See it, feel it, believe in it. Make your mental blueprint and begin."*
>
> **Robert Collier**

Don't be a blank slate. Instead, bring something to the table. Have some sort of end state in mind, whether for the organization you now lead or for a meeting that you hope to steer to some desired outcome. While the vision will change and be shaped by the input of others, effective leaders always have an idea for where they want to lead their team.

A good running estimate, deliberate mission analysis, and the sort of over-the-horizon thinking that leaders do should produce some ideas for where we think we need to go. Teams don't lead themselves. Leaders provide inspiration, purpose, and direction for everything they do. We need to have this mindset before we ever set foot into the arena.

Take Charge!

Take-charge leaders should embark on a top-to-bottom assessment as soon as they are given their new responsibilities. My friends, if we are going to lead, we must know the business. We can't fake it. People will see right through us and go somewhere else for answers and direction. We have to understand the organization, how it operates, its challenges and immediate needs for leadership, and the status of its resources—especially its human capital.

Take time to walk around and listen. I like author and retired Navy Captain D. Michael Abrashoff's approach (in his books, *It's Your Ship* and *Get Your Ship Together*) to taking command by encouraging leaders to first see the ship "through the eyes of the crew." Only then can we find out what's really wrong, know where we need to apply our leadership, and empower people to join us in the journey to solve problems and make things better. Now I don't usually like to give any credence to the leadership techniques of the Navy (just kidding!), but this approach to listening first is what taking charge is all about. Seems contradictory, doesn't it? But too many people jump into leadership without a full understanding of what is needed. They confuse motion for purposeful action and leader *"busy-ness"* for leader *business*.

Instead, take-charge leaders begin by working outward from the organizational "center of gravity" (by now you know this as the B.F.T!). We must understand the main product and the principal contributors to mission success before diving in to other areas. Visit the top salesman, the best performing store, and the main sources of revenue—first. Meet people in *their* workspaces and assess their readiness for the mission.

Prioritize first efforts after taking charge consistent with the importance of those things to the organizational bottom line. Identify and meet with key customers and constituencies. Ask what the organization does well and what it does not do well. Begin to test your vision while measuring the key assumptions upon which it was built.

After a career of being thrust into some very diverse leadership roles, I've developed an approach that has worked well regardless of the specifics of the situation. It's not complicated. Spend time asking questions and analyzing the answers. So often, our teammates have great ideas for how to be successful but need help with implementation. Let them know that you are passionate about excellence and that you are willing to take risks and try new things. Look for gaps—in processes, systems, organizations—and fill them. Put your mark on the shared vision, strategic plans, budgets, organizational charts, people, meetings, and everything else that contributes to mission accomplishment. Quite simply, if we're in charge, then it's our ship . . . from DAY ONE!

Develop Your Leadership Philosophy

Before assuming new responsibilities, Army pre-command training gives its attendees time to refine their personal leadership philosophies. This has been a great exercise, one that I have completed before each new position. I have found that reviewing my beliefs, my core values, and how I will *act* as a leader are critical elements to articulate to my teammates. Doing so from the beginning eliminates uncertainty—with subordinates and those whom we serve (customers, stakeholders, etc.)—and helps define the culture and leadership climate we want to create.

This is what I call the "7 BEs of a Leader." They are the basis for my leadership philosophy and what I hopefully bring to any situation in which I am asked to take charge. You can see how it takes the elements of this book—*plan, prepare, execute,* and *learn*—and applies them to how I *act* and how I view my responsibilities as a leader. This is who I am, no excuses and no surprises. This philosophy is the high bar I have set for myself and what I strive to be in each and every leadership setting. This is the business of leaders in *action.*

1. BE Yourself:

Have you ever considered how totally confused we would be if we followed *every* bit of leadership wisdom we've heard or read—this book included? I'm not sure how we would perform, for example, if we practiced the combined insights of proven leaders like Bill Clinton, Jack Welch, Donald Trump, and Rudy Guiliani—but I'm guessing we'd be a mess! We simply cannot be who we are not.

It is always best to just be who we are. Good leaders acknowledge and understand their strengths and weaknesses and look for opportunities to leverage the former while surrounding themselves with people who can cover the latter. We don't need to change who we are for anyone . . . or anything. While the quest for growth and personal development is a life-long journey, it should not change our true character. Our learning, like our leadership skills and attributes, should be applied within the context of our unique, God-given personality.

What does it mean to *be yourself*? Be genuine. Subordinates can see right through a leader who is trying to be something they are not. Be transparent. Let others know we are human. We make mistakes. We have good and bad days. We get nervous. We care. We celebrate successes and share the disappointment of failure.

Leaders who adopt this principle establish a culture in which individual identities are valued. Strengths and weaknesses are combined to take advantage of the distinctive capabilities of each member of the team. Diversity becomes a characteristic that leverages the special skills, attributes, and problem solving capabilities that are found in different people and different cultures. Leaders ensure that teammates understand that they are valued for their uniqueness.

In business, *being yourself* means establishing a niche, brand, or unique organizational culture. We have our own corporate qualities and characteristics that appeal to our internal and external customers and separate us from our competition. Rather than trying to be like all the others, we need to embrace our uniqueness and use it to our advantage. Stand out in the crowd of business look-alikes. Be yourself.

This is the basis for how we *prepare* others. The focus of our preparation (building teams, empowering employees, and aligning resources to make them successful) is our people. Understanding who they are and matching their strengths with specific mission requirements is the key to success. It is why diversity is so important. Everyone brings something different to the team. Our challenge is to understand what it is and to get the most, and the best, from each of our teammates.

2. BE Positive:

I must admit to being a quick judge of people's leadership capacity. No doubt this comes from four years in the California desert, training Army leaders for combat. One of the first things I look for is whether they have the energy and the passion that good leaders exude. I look for those who have a positive vision, who can communicate it in such a way that inspires the team, while creating rabid followers through a contagious enthusiasm for the mission. I look for those who are positive. And to be honest, I have yet to find a good leader who is anything less.

Charles Schwab once remarked, "I consider my ability to arouse enthusiasm among men the greatest asset I possess. The way to develop the best that is in a man is by appreciation and encouragement." Sure sounds like the kind of leader we would all like to be—and likely all wish we had. We can choose what we bring to any leadership opportunity: Do we tear people down or build them up? Do we hold people back or propel them to greatness? Do we create excitement, view challenges as opportunities, and make life fun? It truly is up to us whether we add energy to others . . . or take it away.

The world is full of cynics. We cannot continue to add to their ranks. We have to choose, every day, to be positive. Effective leaders must be the head cheerleader for their team. They must highlight successes at each turn, finding the good in every person and in every event. Rather than further beating down subordinates after a project setback, why don't we identify what went well, and should be sustained, in addition to what did not and must be improved, through positive AARs? Organizational and personal growth and development can be productive outcomes from our project failures.

Leaders must choose daily whether to be defined by the negative or the positive. "Butt chewing" does not have to flow down-hill! The silly politics, bureaucracy, and mismanagement of our higher headquarters or the front office does not have to be passed along to our teammates. Instead, we can amplify success. We can look for occasions to brag about team victories and the contributions of our employees. We can show appreciation and pass on encouragement at every opportunity.

Leaders have a positive vision for the organization and the type of culture that is required to get there. The bright future that we envision is a message that must be told and retold with high frequency—and high energy. Positive leaders celebrate activities, milestones, and individual actions that enable that future.

Do you see how this impacts each element of our leadership responsibilities? Leaders create positive and inspiring visions, plans, and strategies. We prepare people to be the absolute best by empowerment, support, encouragement, and the appropriate use of their talents. We make them want to achieve greatness by listening to their ideas, including them in the shared vision, and pushing them to reach goals in which they believe. We make continuous learning a part of the culture, turning challenges and setbacks into opportunities for growth. Positive leaders turn failures into future success. It is up to us what we bring to the equation. Let's choose to be positive.

3. BE Mindful of Others:

Leaders genuinely care about the welfare of their subordinates and know that people are what leadership is all about. They put the needs of others before their own. They serve others through empowerment, development, and encouragement. They listen and demonstrate characteristics like compassion and empathy. They know that people have good days and bad—just like they do.

"No man can always be right. So the struggle is to do one's best, to keep the brain and conscience clear, never be swayed by unworthy motives or inconsequential reasons, but to strive to unearth the basic factors involved, and then do one's duty."

Dwight D. Eisenhower

One of the first leadership lessons I learned at West Point was that leaders treat everyone equally. This is not to imply that it is acceptable to treat everyone *equally badly*. I know of several military leaders whose subordinates live in fear of them. One such commander, a friend of mine, never understood what it meant to be mindful of others. He regularly criticized and belittled his teammates in public and created an organizational climate of abuse and distrust. That was hardly the environment that would inspire others to give their best or, in battle, to give their lives. No surprise, my friend was relieved of command in Iraq. His was not the brand of positive, people-centric leadership that our troopers deserved.

So what do you know about the hopes and dreams of your workers? I like to remind people that most soldiers do not join the Army to be lowly privates. They have goals to some day be leading the unit in which they serve. The same goes for our secretaries, staffs, and new hires. Don't think they believe they have peaked. They have aspirations for so much more—and it is our job to help them get there. What can we do to help them achieve those goals? What sort of investments can we make to enable their success?

To be mindful of others is a daily walk in humility. The higher we go in leadership, the greater are the numbers who exist to take care of us. Leaders must turn this around—to serve and not be served, to strengthen and encourage others and not beat them down, to put others first.

Leaders must use the Golden Rule to guide the way we treat other people: "Do unto others as you would have them do unto you." A workplace and a leadership climate governed by the golden rule will have no place for things like sexism, racism, discrimination, or intolerance. Leaders must set and live this standard and hold others accountable. This is not political correctness but rather the living of the biblical wisdom that has guided relationships for nearly 2,000 years. It is the basis for our *planning* (include others in the shared vision and solicit their good ideas), *preparation* (enable their success), *execution* (accomplish the mission by taking care of others) and *learning* (continuous growth and development for *every* member of the team). Leadership is about others, not about us.

4. BE the Best:
The world is full of "good enough" leaders. In his powerful leader-

ship book, *Good to Great*, author Jim Collins states that "good is the enemy of great." Just being good enough is a business killer. Even in high performing organizations like the Army, I am continually amazed at the number of people who settle for mediocrity. They wake up, drag themselves off to work, do their jobs, and head back home. No passion. No energy. No desire to kick the crap out of the competition and win.

Leaders must be focused on execution, on being the best. To do so means having hopes and dreams and daily taking steps to achieve them. Our best requires follow through and the drive and determination to make good ideas a reality. It means volunteering for the project that no one else will touch. Those are the roads paved with high risk—and great reward. It means continually seeking opportunities for personal and professional development. It means taking chances—and taking charge.

One of my bosses would conduct performance counseling with me quarterly and focus the discussion on "above the line" activities. Everything in the standard performance objectives was "below the line," and he had no doubt they would be completed. He wanted to talk about the big goals, the new initiatives, and the wild ideas that would transform the organization. Being the best requires "above the line" effort—from the entire team. Our job as leaders is to get the best from each and every one of our teammates.

Competition is a good thing. Look at those areas that are most important to the organization, those metrics that are central to the success of the company, and never stop striving to be #1. Celebrate successes, and then raise the bar higher. Get out of bed with hunger and passion for making a difference. This is what *execution* is all about and is why we push as hard as we do in our *planning, preparation*, and *learning*. We want to be the best in everything we do. Never accept "good enough"—except in plans, of course! But if you've read everything in this book you already know we never stop adjusting, making shifts, and spiraling in new ideas to transform our *good* plans into *great* performances. That's what it takes to be the best.

5. BE Situationally Aware:

Recall that situational awareness (SA) is the ability to understand one's environment and to be able to make decisions and take actions that impact not only current activities but future operations as well. It is our ability to see first, to understand first, and to act decisively that keeps us one step ahead of our teammates—and our competition. SA truly is the difference-maker when it comes to making decisions and influencing success.

Leaders cultivate SA in their own personal and professional lives as well as in the organizations they lead. It is no accident that the best companies are rarely surprised by an opponent's move, by a legal or legislative decision, or by an industry shake-up. Continuous "scanning" of diverse information sources help leaders understand their subordinates, their customer base, and their operating environment. Information must be readily and willingly shared with teammates to create and enhance mutual understanding of their environment.

SA is not an end state but rather a means to victory. Leaders who cultivate SA within each member of the team are able to leverage awareness into action by seeing first, understanding first, and *acting* decisively. They constantly adjust plans, aligning people and resources before issues arise. They pull in new ideas and are constantly learning. They make quick decisions and out-execute their competitors. They do all this through teammates who stay connected, share ideas and best practices, and communicate with discipline and purpose.

6. BE Fit:

Few areas offer the opportunity to lead by example like fitness. Leadership by its very nature is from the front, always on display. We are constantly being measured, for better or for worse. We simply cannot take the "do as I say, not as I do" approach with regard to fitness if we want any credibility. In taking care of others and in affording them the opportunities to be successful, we need to carefully assess how to invest in their welfare, as well as our own.

This is an area that is ripe for leadership. If we want healthy, energized teammates, we must personally lead the way. We must lead a life of balanced fitness. The benefits of fitness are incalculable. Fit leaders enjoy lower stress and higher productivity. They have the energy and stamina to go the distance, to do what needs to be done to outwork or outlast the competition. They are able to energize and inspire those around them by providing an example of balanced fitness that screams out, "Follow me!"

Healthy employees think and work better on their feet. They generally have higher morale. They are less likely to miss work due to illness, placing a lessened demand on soaring personal and organizational health care costs. And they present a positive image of health and energy to customers and stakeholders. Physical fitness makes good sense (and good cents) on every level!

Fitness is part of a balanced approach to life and leadership. It represents the understanding that we are committed to the overall success of teammates, not just their work output. It implies that there is more to life than work. Thus a balanced commitment to fitness suggests investments in other components of our lives, including: spiritual fitness (going to church, synagogue, etc.), family fitness (regular vacations, attending our children's events, and getting home early enough to help with homework), and social fitness (spending time with friends, getting rest).

Leadership is from the front. In a life of balanced fitness, we lead by example. And by providing opportunities for health and fitness in others, we change people in meaningful, life-changing ways, preparing them for the mission and giving them what they need to go the distance. When you think about it, these are fundamental leadership responsibilities: be the best, improve the team, and leave a legacy.

7. BE Going Somewhere:

Nothing makes a bigger difference in the life of a ship and her crew than a captain who knows where he is going. So, let's all commit to be going somewhere.

Successful leaders have personal and professional goals and daily take steps toward their achievement. They carefully craft a shared organizational vision, embraced by the team, and tell it over and over again—with passion, energy, and commitment.

This is what we expect from our leaders: know where you are going and inspire others to go along with you. So let's figure out where that somewhere is and step out. We need to be bold, take risks, and give people something to get excited about. As leaders, we have to be the ones to look over the horizon and determine what it will take to sustain success. It is our unique responsibility to position the team and ourselves accordingly.

John F. Kennedy said we were going to the moon. Then he led a nation to that end. Martin Luther King, Jr. said he had a dream. Then he translated those dreams into action and and inspired a generation. Ronald Reagan told the Soviets to "Tear down that wall." Steve Jobs said he'd change the way people listen to music. Leaders know where they are going. And then

> *"The secret of getting ahead is getting started. The secret of getting started is breaking your complex overwhelming tasks into small manageable tasks, and then starting on the first one."*
>
> **Mark Twain**

they embrace the various leadership responsibilities that we have discussed here, jump into the arena, and turn dreams into action.

Ask my kids what leaders do and they will tell you, "They tell people to do stuff." Leaders give regular guidance and direction— each an opportunity to align the team with the vision. Every decision provides an opportunity to tell our employees, "We can't build this work of art, this company, this team, without you and your unique contributions. This is where we are going . . . and I need you with me."

That's the kind of leader I want to be. I want to always get better, to strive to be the best, to position my team for greatness now and into the future. I want to take the bold risks that excite people, that get them out of bed in the morning ready to do something truly meaningful. I want to be going somewhere.

When I arrived at the NTC to serve as Sidewinder 7, I took a few weeks to understand what my responsibilities were, meet my team, and complete my first training rotation: preparing 500 engineers for combat. As I mentioned earlier in these pages, by the end of my first month I had a list of 10 things that I thought we needed to pursue. These were issues that I had identified in talking to others and seeing where the opportunities for excellence might be found. They were a combination of short term (early wins) and long-term goals.

One of the 10 actions on my list was to establish a National Center of Excellence for road-side bombs (Improvised Explosive Devices, or IEDs) at the NTC. At this point in the war, it was clear that these insidious explosive devices would be a problem for our military forces in Iraq and Afghanistan. (In fact, they would ultimately become the number one killer on the battlefield.) I knew we needed to get ahead of the problem and set the conditions for training accordingly. I could see with perfect clarity where we needed to be and what it would take to get there. Nothing was going to stop us in the pursuit of this lofty goal.

With some convincing and constant communication (again, the *drumbeat*), the team rallied around this shared vision. We worked hard and held each other accountable. We *made* it happen. In just over a year, we established a multi-million dollar training facility and were soon responsible for the preparation of thousands of Soldiers and Marines to deal with IEDs in combat. It took a lot of hard work by some great warriors. But it started with a big idea, a positive, inspiring vision for where we were going, and my teammates' belief that we could do it. Add in continuous learning and sweat equity and you can see how we reached our goals. I was proud of what we accomplished.

Captain Timothy Vail, one of my junior officers and a real bulldog of a trainer, shared his thoughts with me as he prepared to ship out to his next posting. He admitted that he was skeptical at first of what we were trying to do. He thought it was too much and that we had our hands full just doing our regular jobs as trainers. As he left, he wanted everyone to know that he was a believer. He looked back with amazement at what we had accomplished as the big ideas, especially the IED training center, became reality. Tim's biggest compliment was in telling me that he had learned that one person *could* change the Army. One person with passion and commitment and vision could truly make a difference.

Of course, it took a lot more than just one person. But this is what the business of leaders is all about. It is possible to change the world through other people who share our vision and passion for excellence. Leaders who embrace the sort of philosophical underpinnings that I have described here and invest in the responsibilities of *planning, preparation, execution,* and *learning* really *can* make a difference. And it really does ultimately come down to leadership. If you're the one in charge, be in charge! Your troops are counting on you. That's . . . *Leader Business!*

About the Author

Tom Magness is a 25+ year career U.S. Army officer. He is a graduate of the Military Academy at West Point, has a Masters Degree from the University of Texas, and is an Army War College fellow. His portfolio also includes a variety of military schools, including Airborne training and the Army Ranger school, and professional certifications, including a Professional Engineer license and accreditation in LEED (Leadership in Energy and Environmental Design).

A student of "leader business" since entering the Military Academy at West Point in 1981, the author has led organizations from platoon to brigade in assignments that spanned the world. In each position he has consistently been recognized as the top leader among a very competitive and capable group of equally distinguished officers. He has taught emerging leaders as a faculty member at West Point for two years. He has served as a coach/teacher/mentor/consultant at the U.S. Army's National Training Center for four years, preparing soldiers and leaders for combat. His observations on leadership have been validated during tours of duty as Commanding Officer/CEO for Army Corps of Engineers districts in Detroit, Michigan; Los Angeles, California; and Kabul, Afghanistan. These high level leadership positions with up to 800 civilians and annual budgets in excess of $2B have demonstrated the validity of his military leadership lessons and their applicability to the "real world."

A career as an officer in the United States Army, and a continual quest to understand the relationship between business and the military, has convinced him of one thing: business is nothing like combat, nothing like Ranger training (thankfully), and nothing like preparing soldiers for battle. He has confirmed, however, that leadership is leadership.

An accomplished writer, energetic speaker, and personal coach, the author has completed several dozen articles in a variety of publications on topics ranging from engineering to wetland preservation to leadership. His "Leader Business" blog has helped shape a growing list of clients and emerging leaders in a diversity of fields and professions.

A husband and father of two girls, he attempts daily to employ his "battle-tested leadership strategies," whether in his current position or, along with his wife Michelle, co-leading his beautiful family. And while his subordinates may hesitate to point out his leadership shortcomings, his family has no such difficulty! They keep him humble enough to know that, regardless of one's accomplishments, the business of leaders is a continual work in progress.